GREAT LIVES IN BRIEF

A New Series of Biographies

ACCURACY

BREVITY CLARITY

MULTUM
IN PARVO

These are BORZOI BOOKS

Published by ALFRED A. KNOPF *in New York*

ROBERT E. LEE

Robert E. Lee

A GREAT LIFE IN BRIEF

BY

Earl Schenck Miers

New York   ALFRED A. KNOPF   1956

L. C. catalog card number: 55–9295

© Earl Schenck Miers, 1956

THIS IS A BORZOI BOOK,
PUBLISHED BY ALFRED A. KNOPF, INC.

FIRST EDITION

FOR

EDITH

INTRODUCTION

THE READER who wishes to understand in detail the military exploits of Robert E. Lee does not consult a volume of this scope. That need has been adequately filled by the four volumes of Douglas Southall Freeman's *R. E. Lee* and the three volumes of his later work, *Lee's Lieutenants*. Conceivably, even after perusing Dr. Freeman's painstaking studies, there may be those who feel they have not seen Lee in complete objectivity; but they may turn with real pleasure to the three volumes in which Bruce Catton re-creates the story of the Army of the Potomac. There *was* another side.

True, it is impossible to tell the story of Lee without relating the story of the Great American Conflict, in which he was a principal actor. The years in which Lee was significant upon the American scene are those from 1861 to 1865; before, there is indeed the question of the influences that made him not only a Virginian, but also a particular kind of Virginian; and afterward there is satisfaction in the sweet, mellow respite he found as a college president.

The South, in making Lee the symbol of all the desperate idealism that once supported the Lost Cause, has tended to destroy Lee, that intensely interesting man. Yet Lee, in life, was forced to a peculiar and narrow choice—one for which, bluntly, other men in other times and other climes would have died on the gallows. Instead, Lee emerged a hero, respected and revered by friend and foe. Why? Surely, part of the answer rests within the remarkable personality of Lee. But what else? Within the spirit of that general quality we call the American Character? Perhaps within the very nobility of the once-hated enemy?

For the biographer who seeks the essence of Lee, these are trails fascinating to explore.

CONTENTS

ROBERT E. LEE

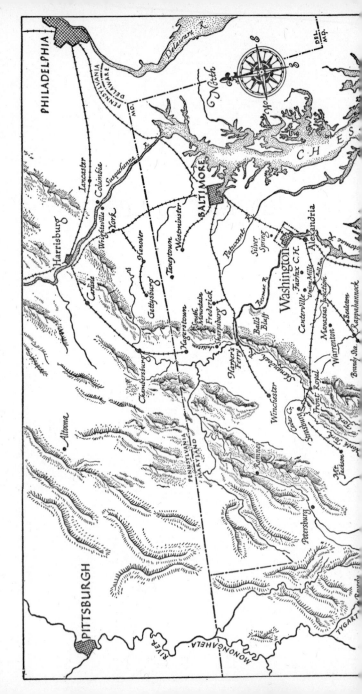

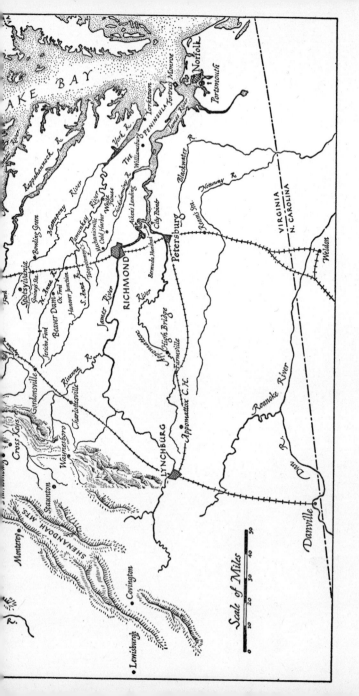

CHESAPEAKE BAY

Norfolk
Portsmouth
Fortress Monroe
Yorktown
Williamsburg
THE PENINSULA
York R.
James River

Rappahannock R.
Mattapony R.
Pamunkey River
Aikin's Landing
City Point
Blackwater R.
Nottoway R.
VIRGINIA
N. CAROLINA
Weldon

Bowling Green
Spottsylvania
Guiney's Sta.
N. Anna R.
Beaver Dam
Ox Ford
Hanover Junction
Mechanicsville
Cold Harbor
Tolopotomy Cr.
White Ho.
Chickahominy R.
RICHMOND
Bermuda Hundred
Petersburg
Ream's Sta.

Ford
Jericho Ford
S. Anna R.
James River
Appomattox River
High Bridge
Rice's
Farmville
APPOMATTOX C.H.

Gordonsville
Charlottesville
Rivanna R.
LYNCHBURG

Cross Keys
Waynesboro
Staunton
SHENANDOAH MTS
Monterey
Covington
Roanoke River
Dan R.

Lewisburg
Danville

Scale of Miles
0 10 20 30 40 50

CHAPTER ONE

TEARS OF BLOOD

THE FICKLE mood of April persisted. Warm days suddenly turned chilly, and often, as the gray clouds gathered, thunder rumbled in the distant hills. The changing temper of nature was sharply reflected along the river. During the bright morning the Potomac soaked up the sun and hardly a ripple disturbed its placid surface; then, with the darkening sky, mists were drawn like shawls around the shoulders of the river, and windswept water swirled and hissed against the pilings of the bridge joining Washington City and Arlington Heights. Deep and allpervading grew this restlessness; it had lasted for weeks. Men traveling the bridge and river seemed beset by the same ominous uneasiness, the same withdrawal into somber countenance and hostile spirit.

In the late afternoon of April 18, 1861 a lone horseman rode slowly across the bridge toward the Virginia bank of the Potomac. The perceptive observer would have guessed from the graceful way he handled the horse and from the tanned, roughened texture of his skin that a large part of his life had been lived outdoors and that recently he had returned from the deep South, perhaps from Texas or the Florida peninsula. His presence was distinguished, yet austere; and the officer's uniform he wore may have contributed to the impression of an unbending, formal manner. He was closeshaven, except for a heavy dark mustache. Outwardly he looked cool and collected, but beneath the thick brows his brown eyes were liquid and tormented.

Robert E. Lee could feel the dampness from the river. Upon the planks of the old bridge the horse clopped

heavily. If, with each beat, the hoofs rang out the words
heart and mind, duty and honor, these words expressed
the struggle that for months had raged within Lee. Now
he approached the crisis: he must make a choice. Yet
there was still one hope, perhaps desperately thin, to
which he clung with the will of a man who had prac-
ticed piety through a lifetime. He was not ashamed to
pray. If Virginia did not secede, his dilemma ceased. For
more than thirty years he had served in the United States
Army; he had no wish to sever this tie, no desire to renounce this love. The events of the day had been against
him. A man could know hell on earth.

Sunshine had drenched Washington when that morning Lee hitched his horse to the post before 1651 Pennsylvania Avenue. The red brick of the State, War, and
Navy Building across the street appeared less drab in the
forenoon brightness. Within that structure toiled the new
men whom Lincoln had brought to Washington—
Simon Cameron, the Republican despot from Pennsylvania who had forced his way into office as Secretary of
War while Lincoln, making the reluctant appointment,
wondered what the people would think henceforth of
"honest old Abe"; irritable, gloomy Gideon Welles,
New England bred Secretary of the Navy; and William H. Seward, with his huge ears and small, woman-
ish neck, who brought to his duties as Secretary of State
a weakness for cigars, cynicism, and abolition. No three
men could have symbolized better the new look in
Washington that had chilled the blood of the South.

Fortunately, Lee's business that morning involved
none of this trio. He followed a code that was becoming
rare in Washington, for he still dared to believe that soldiering and politics did not mix. He turned instead to
1651, where the name plate on the door read: Francis P.
Blair, Sr.

The Blairs were a Missouri family, and Lee, who had served as an army engineer in St. Louis, knew the son better than he did the old man. Both Blairs were public figures of respectable proportions—Francis senior as the former editor of the *Congressional Globe*, and Montgomery as Postmaster General in Lincoln's Cabinet. Lee had no reason to doubt that he was dickering with top brass, and, indeed, the pipelines in Washington had been steaming to bring about this meeting. Montgomery Blair had been to see Lincoln, the senior Blair had talked to the President, his own son, and Cameron, and General Scott had seen John Lee, a cousin who actually had arranged for the present interview.

About what? That question doubtless robbed the morning of much of its cheerfulness for Robert E. Lee. He could not possibly understand what was behind all this maneuvering within channels, except that it posed a basic decision any fool could guess. Six days before, Fort Sumter had been bombarded and two days later surrendered. Within twenty-four hours Lincoln had asked for seventy-five thousand troops. War had come and Washington intended to count military noses—in this case, the nose of Robert E. Lee, who less than a month ago had accepted, in a commission signed by Abraham Lincoln, a rise in rank to colonel.

If Lee could not know all the talking and second-guessing that lay behind this summons, he in turn possessed secrets that would have surprised the Blairs. Mid-March had brought Lee a letter from L. P. Walker, the Confederate Secretary of War. The South authorized no rank higher than brigadier general, but that rank, Walker wrote, was proffered to Lee, who need only "sign before a magistrate the oath of office herewith and forward the same, together with your letter of acceptance to this office." If Lee ever replied to Walker, no copy of the answer has been found. The lesser rank, offered by Lincoln, came later. Lee had accepted that without hesitancy. Just twenty-one days had passed since the hand that had written this acceptance now lifted the knocker on Blair's door. How incredible the fact seemed!

Those early days of April, when Lee's spirits had grown so buoyant, suddenly belonged to almost another lifetime. Yet as late as April 4 the Virginia Convention had taken a test vote on secession, and nothing could have pleased Lee more than the solid two-to-one majority that had lined up against this fatal step. "Secession is revolution," Lee had declared when in December hot-headed South Carolina, spoiling for a fight, had started the parade of states into the Confederacy. In January, Mississippi, Florida, Alabama, Georgia, and Louisiana had joined the Rebel procession, and Lee had writhed at what was happening to the South. "As far as I can judge by the papers," he had written his family from Texas, where he was then stationed, "we are between a state of anarchy and a civil war. May God avert us from both." And he wrote to his son Custis: "I am not pleased with the course of the 'Cotton States,' as they term themselves. . . . One of their plans seems to be the renewal of the slave trade. That I am opposed to on every ground."

As a stanch Southern Whig, Lee doubtless read the editorials of Horace Greeley, and the echo of Greeley's stubborn sentiments was in another letter to Custis: "A Union that can only be maintained by swords and bayonets, and in which strife and civil war are to take the place of brotherly love and kindness, has no charm for me." If, during this period, friends felt that Lee appeared disturbed to the point of illness, a distant cousin, Markie Williams, would hear why: "I wish for no other flag than the 'Star spangled banner' and no other air than

'Hail Columbia.' " Texas just then proved scarcely the ideal environment for the anguished Lee; on February 1 it also seceded. Lee came home to Arlington Heights, a badly shaken man who muttered that slavery was "a moral and political evil." The attitude of reasonable moderation that pervaded Virginia restored his hope. He was brighter, refreshed, almost gay—and quite unprepared for the staggering blow that smote him with the attack on Sumter.

Why had the South acted so precipitately? What harm could the Federals do, sitting in their fort and committing no act more aggressive than sending to Charleston for provisions so that they wouldn't all starve? Why this firing of the first shot, this act of impatience that produced an undeclared war, defeated the position of those in the North who wanted only peace, and overshadowed whatever legal basis the Confederacy had in its constitutional argument with the national government? These were the questions Lee could not avoid asking, never seeing himself as the symbol of the spark that really had ignited the war. Could the Confederacy afford to let Lee hesitate—to let Virginia hesitate—so that as tempers cooled, a spirit of conciliation might find some compromise that would spare the Union? What enemy threatened the existence of the Confederacy as much as patience? In order simply to endure, the secessionists were forced to be headstrong, confident, filled with brag and bluster.

Even as Lee waited for Francis Blair, Sr., to answer his knock, the Virginia Convention was meeting in secret session in Richmond. Would the Old Dominion keep its head and remain with the Union, or would the fire-eaters shout down reason? With this question heavy on Lee's mind, he sat down to the long interview with Blair. The testimony of Lincoln's secretaries, Nicolay and Hay, is that the President had authorized Blair merely to "ascertain Lee's intentions and feelings." But Blair had also seen Cameron, who was anxious to have the experienced Lee take command in the field, and this was the offer Blair made, giving the clear impression that he spoke for Lincoln. Lee sat stiffly in his colonel's uniform; it was true that he was an officer in the United States Army, but he was also a Virginian, not the easiest of distinctions to make to a Blair of Missouri. In later years Lee supplied Maryland's Senator Reverdy Johnson with a terse summary of that painful interview:

. . . I never intimated to any one that I desired the command of the United States Army; nor did I ever have a conversation with but one gentleman, Mr. Francis Preston Blair, on that subject, which was at his invitation, and, as I understood, at the instance of President Lincoln. After listening to his remarks, I declined the offer he made me, to take command of the army that was to be brought into the field; stating, as candidly and as courteously as I could, that, though opposed to secession, and deprecating war, I could take no part in an invasion of the Southern states.[1]

When again Lee stood in front of 1651 Pennsylvania Avenue, his ordeal was far from ended. Clearly now his duty was to see General Winfield Scott, the general-in-chief, and state his decision. Lee hated the prospect of this interview even more than he had disliked the meeting with Blair. His earliest army service had been under Scott during the War with Mexico, and his affection for the old soldier was deep. Some saw Scott as pompous in his liking for dressy uniforms, a few called him arrogant and even senile, others retained the bitterness of the 1852 campaign when Scott had opposed Pierce for the Presidency; but though Scott's advanced years made it risky

[1] The date of this letter was February 25, 1868.

for him any longer to mount a horse, there was fire in the spirit with which, since the closing days of the Buchanan administration, he had cracked heads together to whip his army into trim for the emergency Sumter had posed. Lee knew the real Scott, the soldier of unflinching integrity who was also a kindly old man with great depths of feeling. Disappointment, and perhaps pain, would show in Scott's eyes. Reluctance marked each step that carried Lee across the avenue to the general's office.

Scott also was a Virginian, raised on a plantation fourteen miles from Petersburg. His army service covered almost half a century, beginning with the War of 1812, and including even the abortive Black Hawk War that had swept the prairies of Illinois twenty years later. Here Scott, who did all things with gusto—at the age of nineteen he had stood six feet five and weighed 230 pounds—had won a kind of enduring fame for one of his orders. The general, finding a number of his farm-boys-turned-soldiers drunk on duty, put each to digging a grave his own size. Few army commands ever had been more imaginatively explicit: anyone who continued his wanton drinking knew where his days would end. The War with Mexico had made Scott the father-mentor with the West Pointers of Lee's generation: for all they had studied Napoleon, Hannibal, Cæsar, what practical combat knowledge they possessed stemmed from Scott— the strategy of flank attack, careful reconnaissance, an enemy caught by surprise. Scott was the most solid army man Lee ever had known; solid, too, in that he could not be budged from a fixed idea. But neither could Lee.

Lee, the Virginian, related the substance of the Blair interview to Scott, the Virginian. The old man's distress was as deeply moving as Lee had feared. "You have made the greatest mistake of your life," the general cried. Then, characteristically, Scott became the practical army man. "If you propose to resign," he said, "it is proper that you do so at once; your present attitude is equivocal."

It was a difficult moment for both men. Lee saw nothing equivocal in his position: he opposed secession, disliked slavery, and believed in the Union. The United States Army had been his life—he had no wish to leave it. But perhaps Scott was more informed than Lee on how far events had moved in Virginia. Probably, shaking hands, Scott knew that he and Lee parted forever. A report from Richmond, which must have been known in the War Department, said that the Virginia Convention already had passed an ordinance of secession. There were rumors that three ships had been sunk in the mouth of the Elizabeth River, an act, if it was true, certain to make Scott's blood boil. Both stories, unverified, would appear that evening in the *Washington Star*.

Yet Lee, uninformed of either rumor, left Scott still clinging to the hope that Virginia would not secede. Smith Lee, an older brother who had made a career in the navy, was stationed in Washington, and Robert took his problem to him. Smith could understand both sides of the conflict as the soldier in Lee struggled with the Virginian. Smith's realistic mind, moreover, could simplify the struggle. Home, family . . . to Lee the state across the Potomac *was* his country, his fatherland. But Smith agreed that Robert need not resign—at least not until the brothers had talked again or the position of the Virginia Convention became clear.

Such were the events and problems, that late afternoon of April 18, 1861, which burdened the lone horseman crossing the bridge to Arlington Heights. On the summit of a hill commanding a sweeping view of river and capital stood his gracious mansion. Understandably, the horseman looked with pride at this fine home that had succeeded in capturing the dignity, strength, simplicity, and grace of Greek revivalism. He took the carriage road up the hill.

A restless night followed. With morning Lee set off for Alexandria, saying that he had bills to pay, but the strain he suffered could not be mistaken. He was in John Mosby's drugstore when he saw the newspapers. The bold words: *Virginia Secedes,* struck at him like a whip. Disheartened, he told the druggist: "I am one of those dull creatures that cannot see the good of secession," and Mosby wrote the remark in his ledger beside the entry of the amount that Lee had paid him. Then, with bowed head and folded paper, Lee began the journey home to Arlington.

That evening every room in the mansion on Arlington Heights was lighted; it was like any night, and there were many guests. Lee tried to escape: walking among the dark, silent trees, he confided to the restless wind from across the Potomac his doubts and fears, the image he saw of himself as a man and the compromises that expediency forced upon him. Later he was heard in the bedroom upstairs, pacing the floor. The four-poster with its canopy, the shaving stand with its blue and white china pitcher and basin, the mahogany frame with three steps for getting into bed, dresser and mirror, fireplace and screen . . . these were the familiar objects he saw, the possessions of a steady, quiet life. War would mean that Arlington would be occupied, the mansion seized and perhaps destroyed. Yet Lee no longer hesitated. The letter to Secretary Cameron required no more than a single formal sentence: "I have the honor to tender the resignation of my commission as Colonel of the 1st Regt. of Cavalry." But what could he write to Scott?

Really, there was nothing to tell the old general but the simple truth: "I would have presented [my resignation] at once, but for the struggle it has cost me to separate myself from a service to which I have devoted all the best years of my life and all the ability I possessed." And even Scott could no longer say that his attitude was equivocal: "Save in defence of my native State, I never desire again to draw my sword."

Mrs. Lee thought that she heard Robert kneeling in prayer. It was past midnight when the bedroom door opened. Lee's tread sounded on the stairs—down the thirteen steps to the landing, and then, more slowly, down another thirteen steps. His glance swept across his wife's anxious face. Behind her stood the family dining-room, where they had first courted; adjoining was the family parlor, where they had been married.

"Well, Mary," Lee said, "the question is settled. Here is my letter of resignation and a letter I have written General Scott."

Mary Lee reached out her hand to him. And she thought, as she later wrote to a friend: "My husband has wept tears of blood."

CHAPTER TWO

LEE THE VIRGINIAN

FEW men in the South ever equaled the position that birth and marriage brought to Robert E. Lee. From the time he outgrew the gangling awkwardness of adolescence, he was a handsome man, reared to the Virginia habit of command, meticulously neat, devoted to a sense of order in thought and practice, disarmingly straightforward, charming in social manner, rigorously loyal to Episcopalian doctrine, and endowed with a tremendous emotional sensitivity. An admiring girl cousin, glancing across the dinner table at the youthful Robert, thought: "He looks like a great person." What this natural dignity and grace, this appearance of distinction and force, this tradition of family that was intertwined with historic legend, meant to Lee has been shrewdly summarized by W. J. Cash, among the penetrating commentators on Southern culture: "In all Dixie, indeed, from 1840 on, only a dozen or so men of the greatest and most impregnable position, such as Cassius Clay, of the border state of Kentucky, and Robert E. Lee, stationed in the North, would be able even mildly to express doubts about the institution [of slavery] in public without suffering dismaying penalty. Not even the cloth of a minister was sufficient protection." [1] So Lee, casting his lot with Virginia for richer, for poorer, did so as no ordinary Virginian. With Washington and Jefferson, his was among the most brightly shining stars in the Southern firmament.

Of Robert's father, Light-Horse Harry Lee, it was

[1] W. J. Cash: *The Mind of the South* (New York, 1954), p. 100.

said that he had "come out of his mother's womb a soldier," and in so far as the remark was made by another military Lee, the family must have known that it was spoken figuratively. When the Lees talked of their distinguished ancestors, they mentioned Lancelot Lee, who had fought with William the Conqueror at Hastings; or Lionel Lee, who had ridden off on the Third Crusade with Richard Cœur de Lion (and whose armor still hangs in the Tower of London); and Sir Henry Lee, knighted by Queen Elizabeth. Once the family's roots were transplanted to the soil of the Tidewater, the Lee legend grew as sturdily as ever. In 1799 John Adams wrote to a friend that the Lee family had "more men of merit in it than any other family." Adams was not stretching the point; two Lees had stood with him at the signing of the Declaration of Independence.

Robert Edward Lee was born January 19, 1807, when Light-Horse Harry was fifty-one years of age and in more trouble than he cared to confess. If no family could claim distinction without at least the semblance of a ghost in its closet, Light-Horse Harry exerted a modest effort toward supplying that need. His fame in the American Revolution no one could deny. The brilliance with which he led the storming of Paulus Hook on the lower Hudson made him a hero even in the eyes of Washington, and Congress voted him a medal. When he was transferred to the Carolinas, his renown grew—in the raid on Georgetown, in the action at Guilford Court House, and in a dozen forays against forts that bedeviled the overconfident Cornwallis into the ultimate folly of Yorktown.

But the closing years of the war found strange mental quirks developing in Light-Horse Harry. He grew resentful and jealous of others, arrogant in manner, moody and calculating in spirit. He was far too thin-skinned by nature to withstand these poisons of vanity, and tragedy followed. Even when political prominence came easily and normally to so celebrated a soldier, including three terms as Governor of Virginia, Light-Horse Harry demonstrated no special gift for statesmanship. His dominating preoccupation in these later years with grandiose schemes of land speculation can best be described as unfortunate; they wrecked the man financially, and so depressed his second wife, who was entering that period of desperate health which would leave her an invalid, that she had little wish for bearing a sixth child when on a cold, dismal day Robert arrived.

Yet worse luck was ahead for Robert's father, and the coming disaster exerted strong influence in shaping the boy's character and future. Light-Horse Harry was too stanch a Federalist to have any taste for the War of 1812, and he became involved (entirely at his own insistence) with a Baltimore editor named Alexander C. Hanson, whose press and plant had been wrecked by a mob that had resented an antiwar editorial. Hanson, however, was determined to have another fling at publishing the *Baltimore Federal Republican*, and Light-Horse Harry was equally determined that he should have it. Mobs roamed the street before Hanson's new quarters, and the old soldier in Lee was galvanized into action. He sent for ammunition and threw up a barricade.

Except for someone who possessed more courage than common sense, the situation was ridiculous. The rioters far outnumbered Hanson's supporters within the building. Firing broke out; one man was killed; and with a sudden display of prudence, Light-Horse Harry, along with twenty-three of Hanson's crowd, retreated to the jail for safety. But now the mob stormed the jail, and a frightful scene ensued. Light-Horse Harry was clubbed and pommeled; hot candle grease was poured into his eyes; and one wild ruffian hacked away, trying to cut off his nose, while another stuck him with a penknife. Weak, crippled, and disfigured, he never regained his health. In 1814 he went to the West Indies, hoping that he would improve in the gentle climate there. Four years later, journeying home to Virginia, he died.

Robert E. Lee had just passed his eleventh birthday. His two older brothers, Carter and Smith, were away, his older sister was in Philadelphia under the care of a physician, and his other sister was too young to help in running the house for their invalid mother. In the Southern phrase, young Robert became the "keeper of the keys": he served as housekeeper, supervised the marketing for the family, managed the garden and stable.

Suddenly Robert was old beyond his years, a boy who faced the duty he owed a sickly mother and who gained in return a rigorous training in self-command. His devotion to the woman impressed everyone, and she called him both son and daughter. "If Robert left the room she kept her eyes on the door till he returned," a visiting relative remembered. He was always cheerful, hurrying home from school, lifting his mother in his arms and carrying her to the carriage, and driving her along the Virginia countryside. Sometimes, passing the Potomac, they saw other lads swimming, a sport that Robert loved; still, he remained contented. "When she complained of cold or drafts," another said, "he would pull from his pocket a great jackknife and newspaper and make her laugh with his efforts to improvise curtains and shut out the intrusive wind which whistled through the old family coach." The principal inheritance that a famous but unhappy father had left his son was this opportunity early in life to respond to a sensitivity that was so essentially a part of his nature.

At the time of Light-Horse Harry's death, the Lees

lived in Alexandria in a modest brick house on Cameron Street. It was not, of course, a dwelling to compare with the home at Stratford, the place of Robert's birth, yet the boy soon adjusted to friendly Alexandria, where the engine driven by the Friendship Fire Company was a gift from George Washington, where docks bustled with the endless river traffic, and horses raced at the Fairfax Jockey Club. In October 1824 Lafayette visited Alexandria, and across Washington Street a banner blazed: "Welcome LaFayette! A Nation's Gratitude Thy Due!" Even a live eagle was enlisted to greet the distinguished visitor, but with all the speechmaking and dining, the Marquis had not forgotten the dashing cavalryman he had known during the Revolution and insisted on paying his respects at the home of the widow of Light-Horse Harry. In later years, Lee found occasion to make a special visit to Alexandria and inspect his boyhood home. More than anything else, he wanted to see if the snowball bushes still bloomed in the old garden.

Although Ann Carter Lee grieved at the loss of her husband, she raised Robert not as the son of the unstable Light-Horse Harry, but as a Carter. When she could, she sent him to the Carter family school and saw that he absorbed those traits of self-denial and industry that had made the Carters of Virginia wealthy and respected. The code of the Carters insisted first on reverence to God and next on allegiance to the memory of Washington, who even had ordered dug the wells whence the citizens of Alexandria obtained their drinking water. Carter shrewdness had so well protected the inheritance belonging to Ann that her money could not possibly be manipulated by her financially inept husband, and so the influence of the Carters was reflected in the bread the Lees ate and in the clothes they wore.

A crisis arose for the crippled widow when Robert

was eighteen, for after an interview with John C. Calhoun, the father of nullification, who served in Monroe's Cabinet as Secretary of War, the youth secured an appointment to West Point. Understandably, the mother moaned: "How can I live without Robert?" Yet her pride was great in Lee's record at West Point; he measured up to everything the Carter tradition demanded. He never "ran the sentinel post," and unlike Grant and Sherman, those rascals later at the Academy, he never sneaked down to Benny Haven's for oysters and beer. He was the model cadet, receiving no demerits, standing second in his class at graduation, and, declared his admiring nephew Fitzhugh, "It was a pleasure for the inspecting officer to look down the barrel of his gun, it was bright and clean, and its stock was rubbed so as to almost resemble polished mahogany." Lee came home in triumph, with a commission as lieutenant in the engineers corps, but within the month this happiness was blighted by the death of his mother.

The strong streak of Carter prudence approved at once of Lee's subsequent courtship of Mary Custis. By Virginia standards, he could not have loved more wisely. Mary was beautiful, quiet, pious, the daughter of George Washington Parke Custis, adopted son of George Washington and grandson of Martha Washington. Aside from containing the lovely Mary, the Custis home at Arlington already had become a virtual national shrine to the Father of the Country and the most hallowed tradition of Virginia. Lee always loved this mansion at Arlington Heights; it was, he said, "a house that one might see with half an eye."

Lee's courtship of Mary Anne Randolph Custis was not without its hazards. She alone of four Custis children had survived the first year of infancy, and thus was the center of parental hopes and affections. She was the "unspoiled" daughter, who looked at life with utter simplicity and could not be expected to understand, by her father's more worldly standards, the taint of financial instability that ran in the Lees. Most likely old Custis often wished he had avoided one of those early visits to the home of a cousin of both the Lees and the Custises where Mary had met Robert as a child and had formed her first attachment for him. But Robert E. Lee was a persistent suitor, and Mary had no ear for nasty, idle gossip. She wanted a June wedding.

After Mary and Lee were married, in 1830, it was not long before father-in-law and son-in-law buried whatever grievances they may have fancied. Lee knew that what gave the Custis home its true magnetism was the spirit of old George Washington Parke Custis, who not only filled all the rooms and halls with Washington mementos but also regaled all visitors (among them Daniel Webster, Sam Houston, and Andrew Jackson) with reminiscences of his early years at Mount Vernon. In 1815 he erected the first monument at Washington's birthplace, and his orations on the subject so dear to him ran into the hundreds. Moreover, he possessed surprising literary skill, and his *Conversations with Lafayette* and *Recollections and Private Memories of Washington* delighted newspaper-readers throughout the nation. Yet it was as a dramatist that Custis excelled; his *The Indian Prophecy*, based on an incident in Washington's life, played the boards for half a century; and other plays about railroading, the Battle of Baltimore, and the launching of a warship enjoyed at least a decade of popularity from Boston to Charleston.

Unhappily for Lee, army life deprived him of much of the time he would have preferred spending in his new home. Service in Ohio and Michigan, in St. Louis and at Fort Hamilton, New York, divided him from his wife

and growing family, but none of these tours of duty was
so hard to bear as the twenty-two months of separation
that the War with Mexico produced. Similarly separated from home, Grant ultimately turned to drink, but
Lee was too self-controlled for that; the bottle of brandy
that he took with him to Mexico for medicinal purposes
he brought home unopened.

That the son of old Light-Horse Harry made his mark
as a soldier in Mexico was evident to anyone following
his steady record of promotions—to the brevet rank of
major after Cerro Gordo, to the brevet rank of lieutenant
colonel after Contreras and Churubusco, and to the additional brevet of colonel after Chapultepec. Scott, on
whose staff Lee served when it was decided to go after
the Mexicans through the port of Vera Cruz, spoke un-
stinting praise for the Virginian. At Cerro Gordo, Scott
characterized Lee "as daring as laborious, and of the ut-
most value"; and General David Twiggs reported even
more glowingly: "I consulted him with confidence and
adopted his suggestions with assurance. His gallantry and
good conduct deserve the highest praise."

Lee's quiet, conscientious manner, his evident ability
as an engineer, his tact and grace in getting along both
with his superiors and with the men in the ranks grew on
everyone. Although Beauregard and McClellan also
served on Scott's staff, the impression they made did not
compare with the impact of Lee; and Reverdy Johnson of
Maryland would quote Scott as saying that "his success
in Mexico was largely due to the skill, valor and un-
daunted energy of Robert E. Lee." To Lee the war imposed a duty to be discharged doggedly and as best he
could, but it also produced unexpected moments. One of
these came at Vera Cruz, when he ran into Smith, his
brother in the navy. A letter home revealed how this
meeting turned into an agony:

The first day this battery opened Smith served one of the guns. I had constructed the battery, and was there to direct the fire. No matter where I turned, my eyes reverted to him, and I stood by his gun when I was not wanted elsewhere. Oh, I felt awfully, and am at a loss what I should have done had he been cut down before me. I thank God that he was saved. He preserved his usual cheerfulness, and I could see his white teeth through all the smoke and din of the fire. I had placed three thirty-two and three sixty-eight pound guns in position. . . . Their fire was terrific, and the shells thrown from our battery were constant and regular charges, so beautiful in their flight and so destructive in their fall. It was awful! My heart bled for the inhabitants. The soldiers I did not care so much for, but it was terrible to think of the women and children.

Lee had no real taste for war. In Mexico he was almost constantly homesick for Mary, the children, and Arlington. On the day before Christmas 1846 he wrote a typical letter: "I hope good Santa Claus will fill my Rob's stocking to-night: that Mildred's, Agnes's, and Anna's may break down with good things. I do not know what he may have for you [Custis and Rooney, his eldest sons] and Mary [a daughter] but if he only leaves for you one half of what I wish, you will want for nothing." Future years would find Lee, embittered by separation from his family, writing other letters at Christmas—in 1862 from the troubled Carolinas, in 1863 from war-torn Fredericksburg.

Soon, however, Lee would be returning home. Young Rob, recalling that event, told a story tinged with chagrin:

There was visiting us at this time Mrs. Lippitt, a friend of my mother's, with her little boy, Armistead, about my age and size, also with long curls. Whether he wore as handsome a suit as mine I cannot remember, but he and I were

left together in the background, feeling rather frightened and
awed. After a moment's greeting to those surrounding him,
my father pushed through the crowd, exclaiming:

"Where is my little boy?"

He then took up in his arms and kissed—not me, his
own child in his best frock with clean face and well-arranged
curls—but my little playmate, Armistead! I remember nothing more of any circumstances connected with that time, save
that I was shocked and humiliated. I have no doubt that he
was at once informed of his mistake and made ample amends
to me.

Apparently Lee was quick to recover from this embarrassment if young Rob was not, for his brother heard:
"Here I am once more, my dear Smith, perfectly surrounded by Mary and her precious children, who seem
to devote themselves to staring at the furrows in my face
and the white hairs in my head." He found the children
"much grown." He was an indulgent father, and young
Rob, remembering the happy years when Lee was home,
drew a tender portrait of the man:

. . . At forty-five years of age [four years after the end
of the Mexican War] he was active, strong, and as handsome as he had ever been. I never remember his being ill. I
presume he was indisposed at times; but no impressions of
that kind remain. He was always bright and gay with us little folk, romping, playing and joking with us. With the
older children, he was just as companionable, and I have
seen him join my elder brothers and their friends when they
would try their powers at a high jump put up in the yard.
The two younger children he petted a great deal, and our
greatest treat was to get into his bed in the morning and lie
close to him, listening while he talked to us in his bright,
entertaining way. This custom we kept up until I was ten
years and over. . . . I always knew that it was impossible to disobey my father. I felt it in me, I never thought
why, but was perfectly sure when he gave an order that it

had to be obeyed. My mother I could sometimes circum-
vent, and at times took liberties with her orders, construing
them to suit myself; but exact obedience to every mandate
of my father was a part of my life and being at that time. He
was very fond of having his hands tickled, and, what was
still more curious, it pleased and delighted him to take off
his slippers and place his feet in our laps in order to have
them tickled. Often, as little things, after romping all day,
the enforced sitting would be too much for us, and our
drowsiness would soon show itself in continued nods. Then,
to arouse us, he had a way of stirring us up with his foot—
laughing heartily at and with us. He would often tell us the
most delightful stories, and then there was no nodding.
Sometimes, however, our interest in his wonderful tales became so engrossing that we would forget to do our duty—
when he would declare, "No tickling, no story."

In April 1849 Lee went to Baltimore to supervise the
construction of Fort Carroll, on the Patapsco River. He
was approached to take command of the revolutionary
forces in Cuba, and really had no need to consult with
Jefferson Davis, who was then Secretary of War, to
know that he had no heart for this bloody work. Then in
1852 he began three of the pleasantest years of his life as
superintendent of the Military Academy at West Point,
but in trying to cope with the problem of Cadet James A.
McNeill Whistler, who matched a happy ignorance of
chemistry with 136 demerits, Lee had to admit defeat.
The artist accepted his dismissal good-humoredly, confessing that he had defined silicon as a gas. "If," Whistler
said in later years when his paintings and etchings made
him famous, "silicon had chanced to be a gas, I might
now be a major general in the United States Army."

For anyone of Whistler's temperament, it was fortu-
nate that his military service ended early. Army life held
little respect for individual taste, as Lee could soon testify.
From West Point he was transferred to the Texas fron-

tier, and though he was pleased with his rank raised to lieutenant colonel, the loneliness of camp life and the futility of chasing Mexican bandits and Comanche cutthroats were poor substitutes for Arlington, Mary, and the children. The death of George Washington Parke Custis in October 1857 finally secured a leave of absence for Lee, who, as executor of the old man's will, found himself involved in so complicated a document that even the army could see no alternative to giving Lee further leaves until the autumn of 1859. These were happy months, marred only by the beginning of the arthritis that would leave Mary partially crippled throughout the remainder of her life. Yet Lee could take pleasure in how well the boys were doing—Custis, in the army, had joined his regiment in California; Rooney had graduated from Harvard, and Scott had gone out of his way to commission him; young Rob was at boarding school. At long last Lee could devote some attention to the plowing and sowing at Arlington before the farm there went completely to pot.

If the Lincoln-Douglas debates the year before had disturbed others in the nation, they had not greatly ruffled Lee. That the destiny of Virginia could be bound to the voice of a country lawyer in the remote backwoods of Illinois, so to speak, was a fantastic concept, especially among the Washington relics in the mansion at Arlington. Lee sensed not the danger that had begun to rise like the mists along the Potomac. On the morning of October 17, 1859 he was shopping in Alexandria when a young lieutenant in the First Cavalry, James Ewell Brown Stuart, whom friends called Jeb, walked up and handed him a message. There had been a disturbance at Harper's Ferry, the orders said; troops and marines were being sent to the scene of the trouble, and Lee was to command them. The gist of the matter, if there was sense to it at all, seemed to be that some fanatic named John Brown had seized the armory at Harper's Ferry.

Lee, arriving at the scene, found the trouble worse than he had imagined. John Brown and his insurgents had been playing rough. The armory, arsenal, rifle factory, and bridge across the Potomac were all in the hands of these hell-bent abolitionists, and six of the party were roaming the neighborhood arresting principal citizens and inciting the Negroes to insurrection. Colonel Lewis W. Washington had been hauled from his bed and dragged off at one thirty in the morning. He was now imprisoned in the fire-engine house of the armory together with about forty other citizens. The servants, likewise taken, had been armed. Lee squirmed at his predicament. If he attacked the insurgents, he might kill the civilians. He called for a surrender, saying in the note that Jeb Stuart carried for him under a flag of truce: "Colonel Lee represents to them, in all frankness, that it is impossible for them to escape; that the armory is surrounded on all sides by troops; and that if he is compelled to take them by force he can not answer for their safety."

Brown had not hidden at a farm in Maryland, planning this attack since June, to surrender to someone named Lee. Brown—"a fanatic or madman," in Lee's report—had avowed that he would liberate the slaves of Virginia and then of the whole South; now, holed up in the armory, and, again in Lee's words, "disappointed in the expectations of aid from the blacks as well as white population, both in the Southern and Northern states," the notorious hero of Bloody Kansas placed little value on life, his own or that of his captured slaveholders. Lee expected the worst, even as Jeb Stuart waited for an answer to the summons for a surrender. A storming party of twelve marines was placed near the fire-engine house.

"Three Marines were furnished with sledge-hammers to break in the door," Lee said, "and the men were instructed how to distinguish our citizens from the insurgents, to attack with the bayonet, and not to injure the blacks unless they resisted." Crisply, Lee described the subsequent scene:

The summons, as I had anticipated, was rejected. At the conserted signal the storming party moved quickly to the door and commenced the attack. The fire-engines had been placed by the besiegers close to the doors. The doors were fastened by ropes, the spring of which prevented their being broken by the blows of the hammers. The men were therefore ordered to drop the hammers and to use as a battering-ram a heavy ladder, with which they dashed in a part of the door and gave admittance to the storming party. The fire of the insurgents up to this time had been harmless. At the threshold one Marine fell mortally wounded. The rest . . . quickly ended the contest. The insurgents that resisted were bayoneted. Their leader, John Brown, was cut down by the sword of Lieutenant Green, and our citizens were protected by both officers and men. The whole was over in a few minutes. . . .

Not included in Lee's report was his reflection when from within the armory Colonel Lewis Washington cried: "Never mind us—fire!" Muttered Lee, the Virginian: "The old Revolutionary blood does tell."

Shortly after Harper's Ferry, Lee's leave expired. He could not have gone back to Texas in a worse mood. Playing hare and hounds with the Mexican scoundrel Cortinas was scant compensation for the cancer of secession that now spread with wild malignancy (as Lee saw it) through the South. He could not escape the feeling of demoralization that crept into the army command. After reading Everett's *Life of Washington*, Lee grumbled in a letter home: "How his mighty spirit would be grieved could he see the wreck of his mighty labors!" And a letter to Custis Lee exhorted: "The framers of our Constitution never exhausted so much labor, wisdom and forebearance in its formation, and surrounded it with so many guards and securities, if it was intended to be broken by every member of the Confederacy at will. It was intended for 'perpetual union' so expressed in the preamble, and for the establishment of a government, not a compact, which can only be dissolved by revolution, or the consent of all the people in convention assembled."

Lee's legalistic arguments were wasted in an atmosphere of hot-blooded emotionalism. Texas voted 166 to 7 for secession. Lee, homeward bound, stopped at a spring for lunch, where he met one of his fellow officers, Captain George B. Cosby. Lee spoke of his "confidence that Virginia would not act on impulse" and confessed "that he had ever been taught that his first allegiance was due his mother State . . . [that] under no circumstances could he ever bare his sword against Virginia's sons." Cosby remembered that "as he spoke his emotion brought tears to his eyes, and he turned away to avoid showing this emotion."

Now Virginia had forced him to act. Honestly he could tell Francis Blair: "If I owned 4,000,000 slaves, I would cheerfully sacrifice them for the preservation of the Union." But the Carter blood was in him—allegiance to a sick mother, even to an ailing mother state, was bred in him. And the Custis tradition was his by marriage—this sense of historic destiny that was rooted in Virginia soil and was hallowed.

So Lee accepted the choice that had been made for him in Richmond. Thereafter he never doubted.

CHAPTER THREE
FAILURE IN THE MOUNTAINS

ALTHOUGH Virginians reacted to secession in a holiday spirit, the older Lee boys, Custis and Rooney, were incensed. The people had lost their heads, contended Rooney, who at Harvard had impressed Henry Adams as that type of Southerner who "could not analyze an idea." Virginians, to the indignant Rooney, were rushing, giddy-headed, into tragedy. Lee allowed his sons to think and to say what they would; he gave his brother Smith no advice and, in a subsequent letter to Mary, said that he did not desire Custis to be influenced by his wishes or example. "If I have done wrong, let him do better," Lee wrote. "The present is a momentous question which every man must settle and upon principle."

Meanwhile the *Alexandria Gazette* reached Arlington with a glowing editorial tribute to Lee, declaring that Virginia had "no man more worthy to head our forces and lead our army" and that there was "no one under whom the volunteers and militia would rally more gladly." The *Gazette* evaluated Lee, the Virginian: "His reputation, his acknowledged ability, his chivalric character, his probity, honor, and—may we add, to his eternal praise—his Christian life and conduct—make his very name a 'tower of strength.' It is a name surrounded by revolutionary and patriotic associations."

Apparently Governor Lechter of Virginia agreed wholeheartedly with the *Gazette*, for a summons reached Lee to report to Richmond. On Monday morning, April 22, Lee left Arlington, and the home he loved so dearly he would never see but once again, and then in a glimpse from a passing train.[1]

Journeying through country where, in coming months, his name would become a legend, Lee was sober and thoughtful. From his limited service in border fighting, from the combat experience he had gained under old Scott in Mexico, what real ability could he offer Virginia in this terrible crisis? He was neither a Wellington nor a Blücher; a Mexico without railroads certainly had taught him little about modern logistics; and, in round figures, he never had handled a field command of more than three hundred men. If he was asked to pit his mind against Scott's, how well could he expect to fare?

But Lee's misgivings seemed to trouble no one in Richmond. On the day after his arrival in the capital he was introduced to the Virginia Convention and offered the command of its forces. "I would greatly have preferred your choice should have fallen on one more capable," he told the Convention, but he added, to everyone's approbation: "Trusting to Almighty God, an approving conscience, and the aid of my fellow-citizens, I will devote myself to the defense and services of my native State."

Testy, sickly Alexander H. Stephens, Vice President of the Confederacy, witnessed the proceedings. His specific mission, in coming from Montgomery to Richmond, was to stress the necessity, with Virginia petitioning for admission to the Confederacy, of the President controlling and directing all offensive military operations. Stephens's first tendency was to look upon Lee with a jaun-

[1] During the early weeks of the war Lee was constantly tormented by what would happen to the Washington relics his father-in-law had accumulated. When, eventually, Federal troops occupied Arlington Heights, these treasures were carried across the Potomac to the Patent Office, where they could be more carefully safeguarded.

diced eye; should Lee insist on a command independent of Jefferson Davis, only God knew what might happen. Virginia offered Lee the rank of major general; the best the Confederacy might make him was brigadier general, a commission he had refused little more than a month before.

Stephens, who already had convinced himself that Lee's military experience did not amount to much, fretted over the extent to which personal vanity might influence him. North Carolina would act with Virginia; doubtless all the border states would do likewise, and Lee's power therefore was such that he could force the lines of the coming battle to South Carolina and Georgia. With a touch of cynicism that came naturally to Stephens, the Vice President heard the Convention president speak "of the sages and heroes of the blood of Lee; of his illustrious father and his great Virginia compatriots; of the unanimous vote of the Convention, making him commander-in-chief; and of their faith, that, like Washington, he would be found first in war, first in peace, and first in the hearts of his countrymen." Lee's brief, modest response and subsequent behavior altered Stephens's opinion entirely:

. . . He stood there, fresh and ruddy as a David from the sheepfold, in the prime of his manly beauty. . . . I had preconceived ideas of the rough soldier with no time for the graces of life, and by companionship almost compelled to the vices of his profession. I did not know that he used no stimulants, was free even from the use of tobacco, and that . . . I had before me the most manly man and entire gentleman I ever saw.

That this seeming modesty was genuine; that this worth which his compatriots believed was real; that his character was utterly unselfish, I was to know as the shades of evening fell upon that day, and he sat in my room at the Ballard

House, at my request, to listen to my proposal that he resign, without any compensation or promise thereof, the very honor and rank he had that same morning received.

General Lee heard me quietly, understood the situation at once, and saw that he alone stood between the Confederacy and his State. The members of the convention had seen . . . that Lee was left out of the proposed compact . . . and I knew that one word, or even a look of dissatisfaction from him, would terminate the negotiations. . . . General Lee did not hesitate for one moment . . . he declared that no personal ambition or emolument should be considered or stand in the way. I had admired him in the morning, but I took his hand that night at parting with feelings of respect and almost reverence. . . .

Virginia's admission to the Confederacy depended on endorsement at the polls on May 23, almost a month hence. Meanwhile Lee faced the enormous task of ensuring the state's defenses and mobilizing its manpower. Virginia covered an area of 67,230 square miles; her greatest distance, east and west, was 425 miles, and, north and south, 300 miles. On the strategic line of the Potomac and the Ohio, her northernmost point was opposite Pittsburgh, and at her western boundary, the Big Sandy River, the distance to Cincinnati was 115 miles. Moreover, Virginia was the frontier of the impending war: she must feel the first blows, the hardest blows, faced with a coast line that the United States Navy might rake almost at will.

Lee needed only eight days in Richmond to sense the magnitude of his task. "The war may last ten years," he wrote to Mary; and again he told his wife: "Do not put faith in rumors of adjustment. I see no prospect of it." All sorts of wild, intemperate schemes surrounded him. One plan was to throw Virginia troops against Baltimore, a bit of dash without sense that he quickly squashed. Act

on the defensive, be not "provoked before we are ready,"
he preached, so much so that elsewhere in the Confederacy the rumor was going the rounds, as the lively Mrs.
Chesnut reported in her *Diary from Dixie,* that "at heart
Robert E. Lee is against us." Lee ignored these mutter-
ings and was far more annoyed with the "bravado and
boasting" of Southern newspapers. Toiling with the problems of preparing Virginia for certain invasion, he stuck
doggedly to what seemed military sense no matter what
the croakers shrilled or the braggarts wished.

The clamor for "carrying the war into Africa" rose
rather than abated, and Mrs. Chesnut next quoted the
opinion that "General Lee will surely be tried for treason. He is blazing out a path behind them in case of retreat. To talk of retreat is treason, disheartening the soldiers." But the detractors of Lee were not judging by the
results he achieved. By the end of May, Lee had organized, equipped, and sent into the field thirty thousand
men. With the Rappahannock, the York, and the James
each constituting waterways to points whence Richmond
could be threatened, river defenses had been pounded together. At Norfolk, where the Gosport Navy Yard had
been seized, and at Harper's Ferry, where the armory
that once had sheltered John Brown was in Virginia
hands, defenses had been strengthened and troops alerted.

Lee kept his head, preparing for any contingency that
could be expected after May 5, the date Lincoln had set
for secessionists to disperse or take the consequences. At
Harper's Ferry, Norfolk, Fredericksburg, Richmond and
Culpeper the recruiting stations were doing such a land-
office business that Lee ordered volunteers under eighteen
sent home even though he "very much disliked to refuse"
these "beautiful boys." The state now had an artillery
school at Richmond College, V. M. I. cadets were per-
forming heroic service in training young officers, and, as

the Rebel War Clerk J. L. Jones would testify, the Southern prayer in informed military circles was that a battle could be delayed until midsummer, for "there are not percussion caps enough in our army for a serious skirmish."

Evil portents began to develop. In western Virginia anti-secessionist spirit was being bolstered by Union aid from Pennsylvania and Ohio. But Lee was too much the realist to give this trouble spot major attention. The place to watch was Manassas Junction, only twenty miles from Arlington, where a Federal advance would turn Harper's Ferry and cut the railroad connections with Richmond. On May 23 jubilant Virginians went to the polls to sanction the ordinance of secession; that day Federal troops moved across the Potomac and seized Arlington and Alexandria. Scott was no fool; he was as alert as Lee to the strategic importance of Manassas Junction.

Jefferson Davis left Montgomery to settle in the new Confederate capital at Richmond, but Lee was not there to welcome him. Riding the rails to inspect in person the situation at Manassas Junction, Lee fretted over the report that Federal transports were in Hampton Roads and that large numbers of troops were unloading at Newport News. These rumors were well founded; in jovial spirit, Scott had sent Ben Butler to the lower Peninsula between the York and James rivers with the observation that "it is just the season for soft shelled crabs and hog fish." Lee could only hope that his general there, John Bankhead Magruder, was hammering together the defensive line that would join Jamestown, Williamsburg, and Yorktown.

Meanwhile Lee inspected Manassas Junction, realized that M. L. Bonham, the South Carolinian, was not the commander for this threatened position, hurried on to Fairfax Court House, where he ordered his flank and ob-

servation strengthened, and deduced that Harper's Ferry
was safe from Federal attack as long as the Rebel forces
at Manassas Junction were substantial. Napoleon had understood that two armies always frighten one another, and
that the best general is the one who can capitalize on the
first panic. Military precepts, if sound, are simply stated.

There was a new mood in Richmond when Lee returned—or, rather, a different kind of tension, for Jefferson Davis was installed in his new quarters. Southern
political temperament was never anything but sharp-
edged and thin-skinned, and indicative of the jockeying
behind the scenes would be the sneering comment of
War Clerk Jones: "Those who expect to reach the Presidency by a successful administration of any of the depart-
ments, or by the bestowal of patronage, are laboring under an egregious error. None but generals will get the
Imperial purple for the next twenty years." Gossips
quoted Mrs. Davis as saying that her husband with his
West Point background and service under Pierce as Secretary of War should have been general-in-chief, which,
by inference, suggested that he shouldn't be President.
Davis, commanding in appearance and gracious in manner, stood aloof from his critics, except that when he
knew who they were, he had a weakness of forming a
lifelong hatred toward them; yet he was a good administrator, a good speaker. Only his implacable enemies
failed to forgive the physical cause for occasional fits of
irritability; an inflammation of a facial nerve cursed him
regularly, and when the spasms afflicted him, he was pros-
trated with an almost blinding agony.

Lee now fulfilled his promise to Stephens and turned
over his command to the Confederacy. "I do not know
what my position will be," he wrote Mary. "I should
like to retire to private life, if I could be with you and
the children, but if I can be of any service to the State or

her cause I must continue." Davis remembered Lee from
his days as superintendent at West Point and respected his
"special knowledge of conditions in Virginia." He
wanted Lee near him as an adviser and friend; and Lee's
suggestion that Manassas Junction needed a stronger general than Bonham was promptly agreed to by the President, who dispatched Beauregard, the hero of Sumter, to
this command.

Lee accepted his new status graciously, confessing to
Mary: "As usual in getting through with a thing, I have
broken down a little and had to take to my bed last evening." He had searched the city for the copy of "Dixie"
she wanted, and "the booksellers say 'Dixie' is not to be
had in Virginia."

Around Richmond the characteristics of Lee became
well known. He liked to ride horseback, detested letter-
writing though "he was not satisfied unless at the close of
his office hours every matter requiring prompt attention
had been disposed of," was scrupulous toward the feelings of others, and, said young Lieutenant Walter Taylor, who had been observing Lee, "in the closing hours of
the day, he would take the greatest pleasure in having the
little girls of the neighborhood gather around him, when
he would talk and joke with them in the most loving and
familiar way."

Lee was comforted by the feeling that his family was
relatively safe. Mary and the girls had gone to Fauquier
County to stay with friends, and his wife worried more
over the recurring lameness in her legs than over the in-
vading Yankees. Custis and Rooney had vented their
spleen against secession and acted like true Virginians:
Custis was in Richmond, an officer of engineers, and
Rooney was a captain in the cavalry. Young Rob at
Charlottesville was a distracted student at the University
of Virginia, straining for some place in the military.

Smith served in the Virginia navy as a captain. Lee prayed for each of them; the hours of waiting were growing shorter.

Virginians should have known the first great blow was about to be struck when on July 4 Lincoln delivered a special message to the United States Congress. Lincoln possessed an unfailing sense of history, and in this message, one of the greatest of his career, he spoke not only to his countrymen, but to succeeding generations of Americans, both North and South. He fought, he said, "a people's war." Toward Virginia, and toward events within her borders in which Lee had played a dominant role, he leveled special asperity. In effect, this passage was Lincoln's own declaration of war—against Virginia and against Lee. Visitors to Arlington in our generation, standing on the porch of the Lee mansion, look down on the Lincoln Memorial, and here, in one glance, are the monuments to the two figures, one South and one North, who would step from the war into history and into legend. On July 4, 1861 the two were locked irretrievably in mortal combat, when Lincoln told Congress:

. . . The course taken in Virginia was the most remarkable—perhaps the most important. A convention, elected by the people of that State, to consider this very question of disrupting the Federal Union, was in session at the capital of Virginia when Fort Sumter fell. To this body the people had chosen a large majority of *professed* Union men. Almost immediately after the fall of Sumter, many members of that majority went over to the original disunion minority, and, with them, adopted an ordinance for withdrawing the State from the Union. Whether this change was wrought by their great approval of the assault on Sumter, or their great resentment at the government's resistence [sic] to that assault, is not definitely known. Although they submitted the ordinance, for ratification, to a vote of the people, to be taken on a day then somewhat more than a month distant, the convention, and the Legislature, (which was also in session at the same time and place) with leading men of the State, not members of either, immediately commenced acting as if the State were already out of the Union. They pushed military preparations forward all over the State. . . . They formally entered into a treaty of temporary alliance, and co-operation with the so-called "Confederate States." . . . And, finally, they permitted the insurrectionary government to be transferred to their capital at Richmond.

The people of Virginia have thus allowed this giant insurrection to make its nest within her borders; and this government has no choice left but to deal with it, *where* it finds it. And it has the less regret, as the loyal citizens have, in due form, claimed its protection. Those loyal citizens, this government is bound to recognize, and protect, as being Virginia.

Seventeen days later at Manassas Junction, North and South clashed in the battle of First Bull Run. Lee remained at his desk in Richmond, though Jefferson Davis hurried off to the scene, raising in the breast of War Clerk Jones the romantic if historically absurd hope that Davis would command in person since "in revolutions like the present, the chief executive occupies a most perilous and precarious position, if he be not a military chieftain, and present on every battle-field of great magnitude." Davis arrived too late to please Jones—the Confederate victory had been won. From Richmond, Lee wrote Mary: "That indeed was a glorious victory and has lightened the pressure upon our front amazingly. Do not grieve for the brave dead. Sorrow for those they left behind—friends, relatives and families. The former are at rest. The latter must suffer. The battle will be repeated there in greater force." Yet Lee could not conceal how he had chafed at being left behind: "I wished to partake in the former struggle, and am mortified at my absence, but the President thought it more important that I should be here. I could not have done as well as has been done, but I could have helped, and taken part in the struggle for my home and neighborhood."

Twenty-four hours after writing this letter, Lee was en route to a new assignment. Unhappily, most Virginians either did not read or did not believe the thoroughly accurate report in the *Richmond Examiner* that Lee had been sent on "a tour to the West. . . . His visit is understood to be one of inspection, and consultation on the plan of campaign." Southern romanticism skipped completely out of bounds; the son of the noble old Revolutionary War hero had been sent to command in the field, and at long last an end could be expected to disappointing military reverses in traitorous western Virginia! There was just enough half-truth in these assertions for Lee to leave in embarrassment and return in humiliation.

The long journey from Richmond to Staunton by way of Charlottesville (where there was no time to stop off and visit young Rob) gave Lee ample opportunity to reflect upon the sad affairs in these Virginia mountains. The people of the region never had held any real affection for the Confederacy, and had enlisted more readily with the Union. The action there had been complicated, but the result Lee faced was simple enough to understand—a small but bitter Confederate disaster had been suffered at Rich Mountain and, except for excessive caution, victorious Union forces under Generals George B. McClellan and William S. Rosecrans might have swept down into the heart of the Shenandoah Valley. The stakes for which the two armies contested were still serious, for the mountain passes and roads of the watershed of the Allegheny Mountains had prime strategical importance.

Rain fell when Lee reached Staunton. When on July

29 he left on horseback for Monterey, it rained again. Some twenty years earlier, returning from St. Louis, Lee had journeyed over this same road as far as Buffalo Gap, and now he wrote to Mary: "If any one had then told me that the next time I traveled this road would have been on my present errand, I should have supposed him insane." Surrounded by "valleys so beautiful . . . scenery so peaceful," Lee expressed the mysticism in him. "What a glorious world Almighty God has given us," he told Mary. "How thankless and ungrateful we are, and how we labor to mar his gifts."

Actually, it had been the Yankees under McClellan and Rosecrans who had marred the beauty and peace of the mountains for the Confederates. What once had been rather a tight, respectable little Rebel army had been broken into bewildered, disorganized, bickering units. Demoralized spirits were met everywhere—defeat and incessant rain were not the happiest of military companions —but that was not the worst of Lee's troubles. Reports clearly indicated that a column of Yankees was making its way up the Kanawha Valley, not far from Lewisburg, and Lee deduced uneasily: "Their object seems to be to get possession of the Virginia Central Railroad and the Virginia and Tennessee Railroad. By the first they can approach Richmond; by the last they interrupt our reinforcements from the South." And a letter home would enumerate other bedevilments: "It is difficult to get our people, unaccustomed to the necessities of war, to comprehend and promptly execute the measures required for the occasion. . . . The soldiers everywhere are sick. The measles are prevalent throughout the whole army, and you know that disease leaves unpleasant results, attacks on the lungs, typhoid, etc., especially in camp, where accommodations for the sick are poor."

Lee was speaking with great restraint when he found

"our people" simply "unaccustomed to the necessities of war." Equipment needed badly in the mountains, and directed to General Henry R. Jackson at Monterey, had been shipped instead to General Thomas J. Jackson at Winchester. The Jackson at Monterey was a fascinating fellow—a graduate of Yale, lover of art and poetry, a former judge and United States Minister to Austria—peculiar qualifications for a commanding general, and yet this Georgian at least possessed the humility to recognize his limitations, a novel trait among some of the officers that Lee inherited. Jackson faced Federal troops already entrenched on Cheat Mountain, an elevation of more than 3,500 feet dominating the strongest of the passes on the turnpike between Staunton and Parkersburg. Southwest of this position, fifty miles or so, was a second turnpike between the James and Kanawha rivers. The general notion was that one or the other of these roads must be used by an army crossing the mountains, but Lee's eyes focused on a secondary but usable road linking the villages of Huntersville and Huttonsville. This road would permit Cheat Mountain to be passed, whence Lee could strike for Grafton, get astride the tracks of the Baltimore and Ohio, and cut Union communications between East and West. At Monterey the judge-poet-general, Jackson, liked the idea for both its imagination and its soundness; speed naturally was required, for if the Federals decided to seize and fortify this secondary road, the plan failed. Lee hastened down to Huntersville to see another of his commanding generals.

General William Wing Loring looked down his nose at Lee. He resented his presence. Obviously he wished that Lee would go back to Richmond. Loring not only had fought in Mexico, where he had been brevetted colonel, but had marched a column across the continent to Oregon, and so he knew soldiering! Loring's conceit would become almost legendary in bringing dissension and disaster to Confederate arms—Stonewall Jackson later charged him with neglect of duty and he virtually deserted Pemberton in the crucial battle of the Vicksburg campaign—but the first indication of Loring's arrogance was to confront Lee. Neither speed nor imagination was Loring's forte; the need first for building up supplies and reserves was his argument for stalling. He was surly, close to insubordinate, temperamental. Lee acted the gentleman. He gave ground. Old Light-Horse Harry must have groaned from whatever eternal perch he watched this unmilitary gentleness in his son.

Lee set up his camp at Valley Mountain. North from the ridge was Tygart's River and the towns of Beverly and Huttonsville, both occupied by the enemy. West loomed Rich Mountain, scene of the previous Confederate disaster, and east rose the Federal stronghold of Cheat Mountain. Now in command of the Union forces there, Lee learned, was General John J. Reynolds, who had taught philosophy at West Point when Lee had been superintendent, and who had lived with his "little, pale-faced wife" in the cottage beyond the Academy's west gate. The strategy of war Lee grasped, but the earnest reality of this conflict between rival knights who were also brothers seemed to elude him.

"The mountains are beautiful," his sensitive nature reported to Mary, "fertile to the tops, covered with the richest sward of bluegrass and white clover, the inclosed fields waving with the natural growth of timothy." The occasional farmer of Arlington added: "This is a magnificent grazing country, and all it needs is labor to clear the mountain-sides of its great growth of timber." Then the Virginian grumbled: "Our citizens beyond this [ridge] are all on their [the Union] side. Our movements seem to be rapidly communicated to them, while theirs come to

us slowly and indistinctly." Finally the general spoke a
word: "I think we will shut up this road to the Central
Railroad which they strongly threaten."

The rain kept up for ten days, and then for ten days
more. Lee, reconnoitering the ground in person, one day
was all but captured by three of his own pickets—better
as a joke than as indication of an integrated patrol. Measles continued rampant. Supply wagons stuck in the mud
and had to be pushed forward step by step. "I have on all
my winter clothes and am writing in my overcoat," one
of Lee's letters confessed in late August. Loring's jealousy
responded with painful slowness to Lee's tact and patience; so, too, did his preparations for action. Men com-
pared their camp to "a Tennessee hog pen" and thought
they were getting the worse of that comparison. The
newspapers, without any reliable advice, glibly invented
stories that elevated Lee to an avenging hero; at the end
of the month his rank as a full Confederate general was
confirmed. He worried over Mary, whose arthritis had
grown worse and who wondered if she dared risk going
to Hot Springs. "It must be quite cold there," he wrote,
judging by his own miserable surroundings. The press
continued to fancy him a hero, and on September 1, still
on Valley Mountain, Lee told Mary the bitter truth:
rain, lack of shelter, measles, impassable roads, "have
paralysed our efforts."

Then from the poet-judge-general at Monterey came
exciting news. Scrambling through thickets and over ra-
vines, two scouts (one an engineer) had found a trail
over which a column could reach Cheat Mountain and
overwhelm the Union's exposed flank by surprise. Lee
decided to take the risk, though the hazards were many
and the full strength of the Federals unknown; troop
movements began on the 9th of September and the ad-

vance was set for the 12th. Five days later a letter to
Mary told the grim story:

. . . All the attacking parties with great labor had
reached their destination, over mountains considered impassable to bodies of troops, notwithstanding a heavy storm
that set in the day before and raged all night, in which they
had to stand up till daylight. Their arms were then unserv-
iceable, and they in poor condition for a fierce assault
against artillery and superior numbers. After waiting till
10 o'clock for the assault on Cheat Mountain, which did not
take place, and which was to have been the signal for the
rest, they were withdrawn, and, after waiting three days in
front of the enemy, hoping he would come out of his
trenches, we returned to our position at this place [Valley
Mountain]. I can not tell you my regret and mortification
at the untoward events that caused the failure of the plan.
I had taken every precaution to ensure success and counted
on it. But the Ruler of the Universe willed otherwise and
sent a storm to disconcert a well-laid plan, and to destroy
my hopes. We are no worse off now than before, except the
disclosure of our plan, against which they will guard. . . .

It was just as well that Lee spared Mary from the
grisly details: of impatient Confederates, firing their guns
as they cleaned them and warning an unsuspecting Federal cavalry detachment of their presence; of demoralized
and insubordinate troops who claimed the mountain
streams were too high for fording; of an assaulting column
that, taking a few Federal outpost pickets, believed
grossly exaggerated stories of overwhelming Union
strength and stopped the assault! Yet the true meaning,
to an observer more dispassionate toward Lee than Mary,
who could hold him responsible for not forcing Loring to
move in early August and who could wonder why the
leadership of the assaulting column had been entrusted to

one so gullible toward enemy braggadocio, was not difficult to guess. Lee had fought a campaign and flubbed. In
Mexico, Scott had worked out his plans and trusted the
details to his subordinates; so Lee had still to learn that
he must pay a price for an imitative style of command (in
Mexico, young Grant had noted how different from
Scott's had been the fluid style of Zach Taylor, improvis-
ing to fit the necessity of the moment). Newspapers that
were ready to hail Lee as a master of the military art had
learned a galling lesson. The disappointment was deep—
though perhaps not everywhere did it reach as far as the
indignation of one Tennessean in the ranks, who swore
that "never were men more sick of Virginia and Virginians."

CHAPTER FOUR

BELEAGUERED RICHMOND

LEE returned to a Richmond bristling with gossip, none of it very charitable. Mrs. Smith Lee, his sister-in-law, called the Confederacy "our little stockade," for with the tightening of the blockade on coastal shipping, realists in the South had begun to wonder if a nation of 9,000,000 whites could sustain a war against an enemy of 23,000,000. Malice underscored the behind-the-fan remarks that Mrs. Chesnut heard about the Lee boys—to the scuttlebutters, Rooney and Custis were being pushed ahead in the army only because of their father's influence.

Loose tongues dealt harshly with Jefferson Davis. Now that Beauregard had become more of a popular hero by adding Manassas to the crown of Sumter, the rumor-makers were telling Mrs. Chesnut "that rather than let Beauregard make a good showing," the President would "cripple the army." The charge that the South had seized upon a constitutional argument to declare its freedom for the real purpose of extending the boundaries of slavery and protecting the "institution" against all moral, political, and judicial persuasion lay on Southern consciences, no matter how vehemently the accusation was denied. "God forgive us," wrote Mrs. Chesnut, confessing her own troubled heart, "but ours is a monstrous system, a wrong and an iniquity! Like the patriarchs of old, our men live all in one house with their wives and their concubines; and the mulattoes one sees in every family resemble the white children." To the angry contention that *Uncle Tom's Cabin* libeled the South, Mrs. Chesnut rejoined spitefully: "Mrs. Stowe did not see the sorest spot. She makes Legree a bachelor."

Lee held himself aloof from such bickering; the morality of secession and slavery, once a constant torment, seemed dwarfed beside the sense of failure he brought back from western Virginia. At times the loyalty that Jefferson Davis gave to those he trusted amounted to damaging blindness, and typically now the President shrugged off the editors and gossips who had soured on Lee. What did they know? Victory would have resulted if Lee's plans and orders had been followed. Of Lee during these hours Davis said in later years: "With a magnanimity rarely equalled, he stood in silence, without defending himself or allowing others to defend him." With Davis's own bedevilments accumulating almost hourly, he could ill afford to lose any good friend and adviser. Shrewdly he decided to make full use of Lee's training as an army engineer, and assigned him to one of the most critical problems confronting the Confederacy—its coastal defenses.

On the morning of November 2 Lee missed the steamer up the James, and a proposed visit to Mary, whom he had not seen since leaving Arlington, had to be delayed over the weekend. But by Monday there was no longer any doubt that a Federal expedition had struck at Port Royal, South Carolina. Instead of journeying to Mary, Lee found himself closeted with the President and the Secretary of War; a Department of South Carolina, Georgia, and Florida had been created, with Lee in command. On November 6 Lee hurried to Charleston, doubtless aware that his selection had not been universally popular (Davis, defying all critics, sent the governor of South Carolina a letter telling him "what manner of man" Lee was). Reaching Charleston next morning, Lee waited impatiently for a train that would carry him to Coosawhatchie, the station closest to Port Royal. Excited rumor pictured Forts Walker and Beauregard locked in a savage duel with the Federal fleet. At Coosawhatchie Lee galloped off on horseback to judge the situation for himself.

The reality proved more disheartening than the rumor. Forts Walker and Beauregard had been pounded mercilessly; the island they defended must be abandoned. With good reason Lee, in a few days, wrote one of his daughters that he had stepped into "another forlorn hope expedition," which could become "worse than West Virginia." The fall of Port Royal threatened Charleston and Savannah, seaports vital to maintaining Confederate credit abroad. For one hundred miles the track of the Charleston and Savannah Railroad bridged rivers down which determined Yankee gunboats could sail virtually at will. Between the Savannah River and the defenses of Charleston, Lee counted less than 7,000 troops, which was like sprinkling salt out of a military shaker; another 5,000 troops, partly equipped and with the skimpiest field artillery, surrounded Savannah. Confederate naval support consisted of four converted wooden steamers, each mounting two guns. Their appeal seemed entirely romantic.

Lee did the sensible thing. He worked hard. He prayed for time. He hoped that a good fright would inspire Southerners into talking less and sweating more in strengthening defenses at Savannah and Charleston, in obstructing rivers, and in constructing an inner line of defenses that he might hold with his scattered land forces. Meanwhile he pleaded with such hard-headed persistency for reinforcements that in time his forces, along a three-hundred-mile front, increased to 25,000.

For sheer energy, Lee set an inspiring example. He was constantly in the saddle during daylight hours, wanting to inspect everything; and Greenbrier, a young gray horse he had brought back from western Virginia, was

on its way to being renamed Traveller. "I have a beautiful white beard," Lee wrote to his youngest daughter,
Mildred. "It is much admired. At least, much remarked
on." Yet one day even the distinguished beard failed to
spare Lee from an opprobrious teamster, who snapped:
"Who *is* that durned old fool? He's always a-pokin'
round my horses as if he meant to steal one of 'em."

A driving schedule was a good antidote for a Lee who,
in leisure moments, could be almost overwhelmed with
loneliness for his family. "I wish indeed I could see you,
be with you, and never again part from you," one letter
told his daughters. "God only can give me that happiness.
I pray for it night and day. But my prayers I know are
not worthy to be heard." Lee had no desire, he wrote,
ever to return to Arlington, now that the home they all
had loved had been "so foully polluted" by Yankee occu-
pation. In early December his daughter Annie received
"some violets . . . plucked in the yard of a deserted
house." Lee wrote: "I wish I could see you and give
them in person."

On November 24 the Federals occupied a portion of
Tybee Island at the mouth of the Savannah River. Lee
checked his defenses—river well obstructed, Fort Jackson armed, Fort Pulaski growing stronger. Yankee ma-
rauders, he thought, might provide some nuisance excitement; he anticipated little more. A few days later he was
in Charleston, studying river defenses there. When on
December 20 the Federals sank some old vessels loaded
with stones in the main ship channel at Charleston, Lee
became curiously indignant, reminding Richmond that
on the anniversary of Secession Day "this achievement,
so unworthy of any civilized nation, is the abortive expression of malice and revenge of a people which it
wishes to perpetuate by rendering more memorable a day

hateful on their calendar." Lee was spouting emotional poppycock and must have known it; any device that sealed off Charleston was sound military practice fully to be expected. From the Northern point of view, the fact that the "stone fleet" closed only one of three channels in the harbor was the "abortive" circumstance.

Lee appeared to enjoy his complete reversal of attitude, forgetting that just a year ago he had been calling secession revolution and madness. Writing a Christmas Day letter to Mary, he referred to the *Trent* affair, which the South prayed would bring an open break between the United States and Great Britain. Mary must not be fooled, Lee warned, by "the bluster of the Northern papers"; the "rulers" of the United States were not "entirely mad." On this Christmas Day, Lee was inclined to see, in his sister-in-law's phrase, how much a "little stockade" the Confederacy had become: "We must make up our minds to fight our battles and win our independence alone. No one will help us." Again he declared that they must accept their home at Arlington as lost forever, adding:

. . . They cannot take away the remembance of the spot, and the memories of those that to us rendered it sacred. That will remain to us as long as life will last, and that we can preserve. In the absence of a home, I wish I could purchase "Stratford." [1] That is the only place that I could go to, now accessible to us, that would inspire me with feelings of pleasure and local love. You and the girls could remain there in quiet. It is a poor place, but we could make enough cornbread and bacon for our support, and the girls could weave us clothes. . . .

[1] An ancestral home of the Lees in Westmoreland County, built about 1730, where Robert had played as a boy. The mansion was sold out of the family in 1828 to help pay off in part the debts of Light-Horse Harry.

Early in the new year Lee inspected the east coast of
Florida; on his return he visited Dungeness on Cumber-
land Island, Georgia, where his father had been buried.
"The spot is marked by a plain marble slab," Lee wrote to
Mary, "with his name, age, and date of his death." The
soldier son, remembering his illustrious soldier father,
walked past hedges of wild olive and among a grove of
live-oaks; he saw roses blooming, tomatoes ripening on
the vine; and, he confessed to Mary, he wished "heartily"
that "the next year may find us at peace with all the
world." The Yankee fleet, reappearing off Charleston,
sent him scurrying up the coast. Another group of stone-
filled merchantmen were in tow, but this time Lee did
not seem so scandalized at the extremes to which the
Northern rascals would go to win a war. From the beach
on Sullivan's Island he watched this Yankee deviltry in
rather placid spirit, writing to Mary: "There now seem
to be indications of a movement against Savannah [the
Federals were clearing obstructions from the inland wa-
terway between Port Royal Sound and the Savannah
River]. . . . Unless I have better news I must go
there."

Hastening to Savannah next day, Lee found that the
construction of the city's defenses had "lagged terribly."
Georgian woods were becoming scented with yellow jas-
mine, redbud, and orange tree; within another fortnight
Savannah gardens would sparkle with japonicas and azal-
eas. February brought the laughter and romance of spring
to this Georgian seacoast. Like an Old Testament
prophet, Lee appeared to preach the alien gospel of work,
sacrifice, danger. In low spirits Savannah residents heard
that guns and ammunition were scarce, that batteries must
be broken up elsewhere along the coast and moved to the
defense of the city, that vigilance must be kept on creeks
where sneaky Yankee dredges might attempt to clear

away the obstructions. "It is very hard to get anything done," Lee wrote Mary, glad for a shoulder on which to rest his frustration. "While all wish well and mean well, it is so difficult to get them to act energetically and promptly."

From Kentucky and Tennessee came alarming dispatches. Forts Henry and Donelson had surrendered—the work apparently of an obscure, cigar-chewing Union general named U. S. Grant. In Richmond, where the Confederacy was changing from a provisional to permanent government, news of this calamity may have been held back a day so that tidings of disaster would not mar the President's inaugural address. An unsupported rumor that the Federals had taken New Orleans, War Clerk Jones observed, made the Secretary of War turn pale; and the pesky Germans, largely pro-Union in sentiment, were "going to Norfolk, thinking, as one remarked, if they can't go to the United States the United States would come to them." On February 8, as though suggesting that an effective Yankee spy system may have inspired this German exodus, a Federal force drove three thousand Confederates from Roanoke Island in North Carolina. The invasion of the peninsula between the James and York rivers was expected hourly; advocates of martial law grew more articulate; and practically everyone hankered to hang a spy. Others wanted the government to run to Lynchburg while there was still time—if not to save face, then at least to save the tobacco in the warehouses, which was worth millions.

A cloud of depression blanketed the once gaily militant South, and in Savannah Lee reacted despondently. The disasters in Kentucky and Tennessee, his letters told Mary, demonstrated that the people "should be humbled and taught to be less boastful, less selfish, and more devoted to right and justice to all the world"; and, with the

loss of Roanoke Island, he feared that "our soldiers have
not realized the necessity for the endurance and labor they
are called upon to undergo, and that it is better to sacrifice themselves than our cause."

The wholeness of Lee was derived in no small measure from the fact that he was consistently the objective
man, attending to duty and trusting in God for his moti-
vation. He never understood the Gallic romanticism of
a Beauregard, the stubbornly contrived legalism of a Jefferson Davis, the political opportunism of a Rhett or a
Pickens, the this-or-nothingness of the South Carolina
nullifiers fused into the Confederacy; an unanalyzed
Cause admitted of no alternative. Of Lee's son Rooney,
during his Harvard days, Henry Adams had thought:
"He was . . . so simple that even the simple New
England student could not realize him"; and this trait
Rooney inherited from his father. Now, when the spirit
of the South began to show the first frightening indications that it might be unequal to sustaining its passion,
Lee never comported himself more characteristically.
Quietly, undramatically, he faced up to his duty in Sa-
vannah, proving, in that inexplicable expression of the
day, that he was "sound on the goose."

Actually Lee could have asked for no more effective
ally in the defense of Savannah than Union General
Thomas W. Sherman, who was cautious to the point of
sluggishness. Yankee gunboats, pushing through the
creeks and marshes, shelled steamers navigating the Savannah River without hitting their mark. Lee worked
steadily on a line of defense at Fort Jackson and believed
that he needed only time and guns to repel the invaders—
and perhaps a bit more backbone in his new troops, who
were easily demoralized by the talk of the overwhelming
numbers the Yankees could throw against them. Writing
to Annie, Lee growled over Southerners content "to

nurse themselves and their dimes" while they left "the protection of themselves and families to others"; and, he added, "if our men will stand to their work," he would give the Yankees trouble and "damage them yet." The Federal objective, Lee guessed, was to open the river to their vessels, but he was ready for them on his interior line. Even as he wrote to Annie, orders were on the way, summoning him to Richmond.

The mounting tension in the Confederate capital surpassed any pessimistic impression that Lee might have gained from the distance of Charleston and Savannah. Martial law had been declared in Richmond, and with fixed bayonets guards stood outside the door of the passport office, suspicious that a Yankee agent lurked behind every unfamiliar crop of whiskers. A Confederacy that had pitted its agricultural resources against the highly industrialized North knew that it wasn't winning a quick war and was handicapped in fighting a long one. More discouraging than the petty betrayal of those who forged prescriptions to obtain brandy needed by the medical corps was the grim realization that Southern emissaries were cooling their heels outside European courts with every prospect of those diplomatic feet growing colder with time. Eight months before, with the smashing victory at Manassas, the Confederates had held a line virtually on Washington's doorstep; now was it true that the commanding general there, Joseph E. Johnston, so feared mounting Federal strength and the possibility that Yankees would sail up the Potomac and fall on his right flank that he wanted to withdraw to the line of the Rappahannock? Lee, reaching Richmond, would find this rumor accurate.

That Davis and his Congress had begun to snarl like angry pit dogs need not have surprised anyone, considering the situation. Affairs were going badly and official

Richmond wanted somebody to blame. Judah P. Benjamin, the Secretary of War, seemed a ready-made scape-
goat for failing to send the guns and ammunition to hold
Roanoke Island. The mood of Congress was such that
even if, without giving essential information to the enemy, it had been possible to admit Benjamin had no ammunition to send to Roanoke, or hardly a flintlock left
in his Richmond arsenal, these facts would have been
shrugged off as an effort to obscure the basic issue with
technicalities. Davis knew how to handle this contro-
versy: he intended to replace Benjamin with George W.
Randolph, a grandson of Thomas Jefferson. But Congress wanted more. Who was the real meddler in military decisions if it wasn't Davis? What was more needed
than a secretary of war with professional training also to
serve as commander-in-chief? Davis thwarted a determined assault upon his constitutional prerogatives by ex-
ercising his veto power; and then, before his enemies
in Congress could regroup forces, appointed Lee, acting
under Presidential authority, to supervise all military operations. Congressional opposition certainly hadn't been
satisfied; it had been stymied. In one paper Southerners
read that Lee had been reduced to "an orderly sergeant."

"I will not complain, but do my best," Lee wrote
Mary when, on the 13th of March, he went to his new
office in the War Department Building at Ninth and
Broad. Perhaps, unlike War Clerk Jones, he did not
stop at the hydrant for a drink of water and so was not
"repulsed" by the tumbler reeking with "the smell of
whiskey"; perhaps, unlike Jones, he did not venture into
the basement to retch at "a thousand garments of dead
soldiers, taken from hospitals and battlefields, and exhal-
ing a most disagreeable, if not deleterious, odor." Rather,
Mary heard of the death of their old friend Bishop
Meade, who, in his last hours, had sent for Lee. The old

bishop called Lee "Robert," and remembered the time when Lee used to say catechism to him. "He invoked the blessing of God upon me and the country," Lee wrote, choked with feeling. "His hand was then cold and pulseless, yet he shook mine warmly." Also, Mary learned, young Rob was in Richmond, staying at the Spottswood. There was no point arguing with Rob; in his present mood it would be "useless" for him to return to college. Lee had gone with Rob to secure "his overcoats, blankets, etc."; as might have been expected, Rob said, he bought "a great deal too much."

So Lee began still another "forlorn hope" assignment, filled with personal sorrow and anxiety and surrounded by a spirit of gloom. Estimates in Richmond placed between 120,000 and 150,000 (some said 200,000) the well-equipped Federal army that at any moment could be hurled against Virginia. There was no cause for believing that this great force would not be used with audacity and vigor; and since the Confederate spies and sympathizers in Washington who had proved so effective during the early months of war seemed to have suffered an almost total paralysis, the South also must brace for unpleasant surprise. Lee's authority was provisional, his duties undefined except in the broadest terms imaginable, and his responsibility, in the last analysis, appeared to be finding how to work some miracle by which impending disaster could be averted.

Panic ebbed and flowed through official Richmond. Lee hardly had assumed his new duties when couriers brought to the War Department fresh portents of calamity. Lee read the bleak dispatch: a Federal force, descending from Roanoke Island, had routed 4,000 Confederate troops at New Berne, North Carolina. Lee's eyes, measuring on a map the distance from New Berne to Goldsboro, saw the sixty miles the Yankees must push to cut the main railroad line between Richmond and the coastal states to the south. Lee acted promptly. At Norfolk, Benjamin Huger commanded 13,000 troops, not much to defend the coast there against serious attack, but Lee withdrew what regiments he dared and shunted them off to threatened North Carolina. Two brigades of infantry and two companies of artillery were nibbled from the right wing of Johnston's army.

If this shifting of forces amounted to robbing Peter to pay Paul, Lee had just begun to play that risky game.

CHAPTER FIVE

THE EMERGENCE OF LEE

LATE March brought even more distressing news from Huger at Norfolk. Twenty steamers had moved down the Chesapeake and were disembarking Federal troops at Old Point, across the inlet from Hampton Roads. Just what this movement signified was anyone's guess. Were these reinforcements for a campaign in North Carolina, for the Federal force already at Fort Monroe, or the advance of McClellan's great Army of the Potomac tensing for an attack at Richmond up the Peninsula? At Yorktown and Gloucester Point, where Major General John B. Magruder commanded another twelve thousand Confederates, the steamers also had been seen, and "Prince John" Magruder, who possessed a liking for amateur acting, did not intend to let Huger outdo him at wringing hands. Lee saw no choice but to stand alerted for any contingency. North Carolina couldn't be thrown to the Yankees to divert their fancy; it must be reinforced, bitterly defended, held. As Lee saw the situation, Huger and Magruder must each prepare to dash to the other's rescue, depending on whether the Yankees struck at Norfolk or the lower Peninsula.

"Prince John" asked what reserves he could expect from Richmond, and learned that at the moment they were few—very few. It was not difficult for Magruder to foresee a tragedy that might not suit his best talent, and, with all the force at his command, he urged a swift exit from Yorktown. Lee was less imaginative, but eminently more practical. Magruder must stand firm and not leave this first line of defense unless Federal gunboats pounded their way up the York or the James. "Prince John" rose to the emergency manfully; on one occasion, marching his forces around in a circle through trees close to the shore, so that the Federals observing him across the water saw a constant stream of gray-clads in motion, he fooled his enemy into thinking he was many times stronger than he was.

In the War Department, studying the maps, Lee's glance focused with increasing interest on Johnston's army, now withdrawn across the Rappahannock and the Rapidan. If McClellan was committed to a campaign on the Peninsula, how much chance existed that he could also mount a serious assault against Richmond from the north? Lee pondered the risk in bringing the major portion of Johnston's army to the Peninsula. Why not? The suggestion, however, nettled Johnston; he didn't believe in splitting armies, his own most of all. Adding to the confusion and uncertainty, Old Joe reported strong Federal activity on his front; and, he said, the five thousand troops under Stonewall Jackson in the Shenandoah Valley (a part of Johnston's army) had found the Yankees far from quiet.

Lee hesitated. At least he could approach Johnston as an old friend, whereas relations between Davis and Johnston steadily deteriorated toward that point where, had either thought of it, each might have enjoyed sticking voodoo pins into the other's effigy. In joining the Confederate cause, Johnston had resigned as Quartermaster General of the United States Army, and could have been considered as ranking either first or fourth among Southern generals, depending on whether he was classified by detail or according to permanent lineal rank. Davis decided to place him fourth, wounding a dignity never noted for its quick recuperative powers. Johnston was as stubbornly argumentative as Davis, as strong-willed, as nervous and irascible under strain. War imposed upon each the necessity of suffering the other, and they did so grudgingly. In late March the diary of War Clerk Jones recorded that "Joseph E. Johnston is a doomed fly."

But Lee did not share this attitude. Light-Horse Harry had fought with Peter Johnston during the campaigns of the Revolution in the Carolinas, so that tradition formed the first bond between the sons of these old colonial warriors. Lee and Johnston had been classmates at West Point and affectionate comrades-in-arms in Mexico. Lee recognized Johnston's ability as a military strategist, understood his capacity for generous, warmhearted impulse, and was willing to deal tactfully (at times almost guilefully) with his sensitive pride. He drew a few reserves from Johnston's army to help on the Peninsula, then a few more. He was like a boy nibbling at the icing on a cake.

April arrived with more reports indicating that Johnston on the line of the Rappahannock-Rapidan and Jackson in the Valley did not feel happy over the Federal strength that could be thrown against them. Additional Union transports were reported moving down the Potomac, destination unknown. On the lower Peninsula a disturbed Magruder noticed the Federals beginning to stir at Old Point, and on still nights Richmond residents believed that they heard heavy guns firing from the direction of Yorktown. Lee continued to work quietly, undramatically, drawing reserves from wherever he could until the forces on the lower Peninsula had been built to 31,500. Johnston's army, including the troops under Jackson and 1,200 cavalry under Jeb Stuart, had been reduced to 28,000—ragged gouges were about to show in the icing.

Again the name of Grant was in the news, this time at Shiloh, a bloody slaughter forcing the Confederates

back from their base at Corinth, for all that the Southern
press claimed a smart victory. Even the most optimistic
editorial-writers in Richmond were stumped to find any
virtue in the capitulation of Island No. 10, which broke
the last Confederate hold on the upper Mississippi. Soon
reports described Davis as looking "thin and haggard,"
but War Clerk Jones took cheer from the rumor that the
President planned to be baptized. Yet there were those,
remembering Cromwell and Richard III, who saw sinis-
ter implications in even this intention, alleging, Jones said,
that "professions of Christianity" were sometimes "the
premeditated accompaniments of usurpations."

Not all of Lee's troubles were military. The remarkable "bounty and furlough act"—a law, one expert declared, designed "to disorganize and dissolve the provisional army"—had been on the statute books when Lee
was called back to Richmond. A bounty of fifty dollars
and a sixty-day furlough were the least of the dubious
plums, by military standards, that this legislation dan-
gled before any soldier who re-enlisted for three years (or
until the war ended). If dissatisfied for any reason, real
or fancied, the soldier might shift at will from one company to another. Whenever a vacancy occurred, he
elected his own officers—a whip that he held over any
young squirt too insistent on military discipline. For all
that the "bounty and furlough act" and supporting legislation coddled the enlistee, it was not filling Confederate
ranks as service terms expired.

Lee felt uneasy, realizing that as the emergency confronting the Confederacy mounted, its fighting strength
dwindled. The law he wanted was a conscription act affecting all white males between the ages of eighteen and
forty-five. "The whole nation," Lee preached, "should
for the time be converted into an army, the producers to
feed and the soldiers to fight." Congress listened, but

with one ear harkening to political sentiments at home. The legislators reduced Lee's age limit from forty-five to thirty-five, and, bargaining compromises, restored most of the silly features of the "bounty and furlough act" to the new law. Still, a form of conscription had been won.

At the close of the first month in office, the "orderly sergeant" to the President had begun to make an impact, and to many Lee appeared the core of a hitherto badly shaken War Department. He remained calm, energetic, cheerful—even when, one April day, the Reverend K. J. Stuart arrived in worried Richmond, saying that he had just escaped from Alexandria, where he had seen McClellan aboard one of the transports carrying Federal troops from that city. The minister's story, if reliable, ended speculation: the life-and-death struggle for Virginia, perhaps for the Confederacy, was coming on the Peninsula. Lee's mind snapped to the obvious decision: Johnston was needed in Richmond.

Davis's order brought Johnston and his two strongest divisions (under Longstreet and Gustavus Smith) to Richmond; a division under Ewell was left on the Rappahannock to watch the Yankees and co-operate with Jackson in the Valley should trouble brew there; and another brigade remained at Fredericksburg. Not too much could be learned about Federal troops remaining in northern Virginia beyond the fact that they were commanded by Irvin McDowell.[1] An essential requirement of command was the courage to act boldly while whistling in the dark. Lee possessed the temperament for such moments; Johnston did not. "Old Joe" hardly reached Richmond before he produced a new crisis.

[1] Actually what the press now began to call "McDowell's Army" was a division detached from McClellan, at Lincoln's insistence, to safeguard Washington while McClellan was on the Peninsula.

A call from Davis brought Lee to an emergency council of war. A grim group awaited him in the President's office: Secretary of War Randolph, sitting erect and worried; Johnston, flanked by Longstreet and Smith, clearly filled with apprehensions; Davis at his desk, calculating and impassive. Johnston spoke first. He had just returned from an inspection of Norfolk and the Peninsula. The Yorktown line, he insisted, could not be defended for many reasons: it was too long, the batteries on the York could be quickly silenced by Federal gunboats, the nerves of Magruder's troops were wearing thin. Smith supported Johnston; Longstreet, troubled with deafness, was owlishly silent. Johnston argued that Norfolk and the lower Peninsula should be abandoned; troops from Virginia, the Carolinas, and Georgia should be concentrated in front of Richmond, forcing McClellan to fight far distant from his base; or Magruder's force should defend Richmond under siege while other forces carried the war into the enemy's country.

Randolph protested abandoning Norfolk. Did Johnston propose yielding all hope of ever building a navy to contest Federal power on the sea? Davis turned to Lee. What did he think? Lee reduced his objections to two questions. How could any large number of troops be called from Georgia or the Carolinas without exposing Charleston and Savannah to almost certain capture? Were not the fields of battle offered on the Peninsula excellent for a small army contending against superior numbers? Longstreet, listening hard, remained content with his own counsel. The meeting, beginning an hour before noon, dragged on, and "Old Joe," by his own account, was neither happy nor convinced by other arguments:

At six o'clock the conference was adjourned by the President, to meet in his house at seven. The discussion was continued there, although languidly, until 1 A.M., when it ceased; and the President, who previously had expressed no position on the question, announced his decision in favor of General Lee's opinion, and directed that Smith's and Long-street's division should join the Army of the Peninsula and ordered me to go there and take command. . . . The be-lief that events on the Peninsula would soon compel the Confederate Government to adopt my method of opposing the Federal army reconciled me somewhat to the necessity of obeying the President's order.

A troubled fortnight followed for Lee. Johnston, huffed, stubborn and distrustful, still had not asked to be relieved, and Davis confessed that he did not "wish to separate him from the troops with whom he was so in-timately acquainted." Lee, analyzing Johnston's position, must have squirmed. Clearly Johnston believed that in time McDowell would join McClellan in a concen-trated drive on Richmond. The Confederate brigade at Fredericksburg consisted of not more than 2,500 men; how long would it take McDowell to overrun this force and march the remaining sixty miles to Richmond? April 21 brought a depressing dispatch: McDowell's army had begun to debark at Aquia Creek, north of Fredericksburg.

Where Johnston's instincts were those of the slugger, Lee was a boxer, anxious to disconcert his opponent with counterpunches, swift and unexpected. He must catch the Federals off balance. At Gordonsville, forty-seven miles west of Fredericksburg, was part of Lee's counterpunch—Ewell's 8,500 troops. At Swift Run Gap, twenty-five miles northeast of Staunton, was Jack-son's force, now increased to 6,000, holding in check Federal forces in the Valley under Nathaniel P. Banks. Ewell could be moved to Fredericksburg, to Richmond, or over the Blue Ridge to support Jackson—those were

Lee's choices. But Lee already had decided that Fredericksburg must be reinforced by troops from elsewhere.

How much faith could Lee place in Jackson? It was true that he had fought well at Manassas, but later he had lost a minor fight at Kernstown and he seemed to march his men to the point of needless exhaustion. Dick Ewell lisped that Jackson was mad as a hatter, but Ewell's remarks always had to be evaluated in the light of his chronic dyspepsia. In the War with Mexico Jackson had shown some skill as an artillerist, and had been brevetted major for gallantry at Chapultepec. Afterward he had taught at Virginia Military Institute, and undergraduates had nicknamed him "Tom Fool" Jackson. He was now thirty-seven, a man of restless spirit in every inch of his six feet, and his weary blue eyes, looking down over a rusty brown beard, seemed lost in inward brooding. Some said he was a Calvinistic nut who fancied himself the Joshua of the Confederacy; apparently he possessed no sympathy for human infirmity, and men on the march who fainted by the wayside he suspected of wanting in patriotism. Except for zeal, Jackson had proved very little about himself, and yet Lee, if he was to strike an effective counterpunch, had to believe in him.

To drive the Federals under Banks down the Valley, Lee wrote Jackson, would provide a "great relief" to pressure on Fredericksburg. Lee proposed to move Ewell to Hanover Junction, where he had access by rail to Fredericksburg, the Valley, or Richmond. Jackson could call on Ewell if he felt he needed his support in driving back Banks. Both Ewell and Jackson were under Johnston's direct command, but that fact seemed to trouble neither Lee nor Jackson. A campaign in the Valley that threatened the communications of a Federal army oper-

ating north of the Rappahannock would stop that army's
advance on Richmond. Nothing else mattered to Lee.
"The blow, wherever struck, must, to be successful, be
sudden and heavy," he wrote to the gray-clad Joshua at
Swift Run Gap.

Jackson, the man of mood and mystery, disappeared
into the mountains. The moment called for all the cheerfulness Lee possessed, for April ended in a shower of bad
tidings. On the 24th New Orleans, the Confederacy's
richest port, had been plucked like a ripe plum by the
Yankees. Would Richmond be next? Cabinet officers
arranged for their families to return home or to journey to
other places of refuge. The President's family, it was
gossiped, would soon depart for Raleigh. Reading the
dispatches that came from Johnston during the closing
days of April certainly cheered no one. Old Joe had one
idea—to get off the lower Peninsula as quickly as possible. His communications inquired about the construction of bridges over the Chickahominy, speculated on an
immediate evacuation of Richmond, harped again on the
possible counter-offensive of crossing the Potomac and
carrying the fight to the enemy. But if Johnston was worried, so also was McClellan in his headquarters at Fortress Monroe; even after sending scouts aloft in a balloon
to reconnoiter the enemy, McClellan fretted and dallied.
Johnston, however, had no wish to wait for McClellan
to muster the courage for a fight. He gave Richmond
warning on the day before that he intended to abandon
Yorktown on the night of May 2–3.

Davis wired Johnston to stand where he was, and hastened off with his Secretaries of War and Navy to see
what could be saved (ironically, in Washington, Lincoln was preparing to journey to Fortress Monroe with
his own Secretaries of War and Treasury in an effort to
discover why McClellan was so hopelessly stalled). At

Norfolk, Davis countermanded Johnston's order for Huger to clear out of the place, and gained a week's time. Even so, Confederate losses in equipment, in guns, in shipbuilding facilities and heavy artillery amounted to a staggering sacrifice. Davis returned to Richmond, sad at heart, but there was more bad news. Johnston had quit the Yorktown defenses on May 4, and Federal gunboats, pounding their way up the York, had reached West Point, thirty-seven miles from Richmond. On the 5th there was fighting in Williamsburg—brutal, bloody fighting in the rain with the Confederate wounded left on the field.

No one could be quite sure what was happening, including Davis or Lincoln. McClellan had been prepared to bombard Yorktown on the 4th, then discovered the place evacuated. Cheerily he wired Washington: "I shall push the enemy to the wall." But Lincoln, arriving at Fortress Monroe and visiting the camps of the army, found Norfolk still unoccupied and the *Merrimac's* [2] threat ignored. Cussed mad, he slammed his hat on the floor. But if the Federals couldn't make up their minds where and when to fight on the Peninsula, the Confederates under Johnston were equally confused over where to make a stand.

In Richmond, Lee found Johnston suddenly uncommunicative. A suggestion that light artillery be placed at West Point to deter Federal gunboats from penetrating farther toward Richmond went unanswered. Old Joe now had reached Brahamsville, thirty-five miles from the capital, and here, pausing five days, exploded snappishly. Lee was interfering in his command, especially on the James and in front of Fredericksburg, and he was com-

[2] The vessel was burned by the Confederates on May 10, the same day that Davis, baptized at home, was privately confirmed in St. Paul's Church.

pletely uninformed of plans for defending Richmond. "My authority," wrote Johnston, as stiff as the pen scratching out his grievances, "does not extend beyond the troops immediately around me. I request therefore to be relieved of a merely geographical command. The service will gain thereby the unity of command, which is essential in war."

Lee swallowed his own pride to soothe Old Joe's. Archives in the War Department were being packed for shipment to Lynchburg and Columbia, South Carolina—it was no time for personalities to erupt. A mollified Johnston continued drawing his army back toward the Chickahominy, fifteen miles from Richmond. Lee's mind turned uneasily to the uncompleted batteries at Drewry's Bluff, the last defense on the James that could stop Federal gunboats from reaching Richmond. Day and night workmen toiled, strengthening these posts.

By mid-May, Johnston had his army across the Chickahominy, but Davis, riding out to see the general, returned to the capital more troubled than ever. Why was Johnston in the suburbs of Richmond and not contesting the crossing of the Chickahominy with McClellan? Was Richmond to be given up without a battle? Old Joe's answers were far from satisfactory, for Postmaster General John H. Reagen recalled:

The President's anxiety was known to the Cabinet. He invited General Robert E. Lee . . . to meet with the Cabinet . . . announced his solicitude and requested General Lee's opinion as to the next best line of defense, if Richmond should be abandoned. General Lee, after discussing the question as a military engineer, stated that the next best line of defense would be at Staten River. "But," he added, "Richmond must not be given up—it shall not be given up." As he spoke the tears ran down his cheeks. . . . I never saw him show equally deep emotion.

May 15 brought ominous reports. Federal gunboats approached Drewry's Bluff, and if the batteries that Lee had been strengthening and which still were not completed did not repel the vessels, the James became a highway of Federal invasion. Lee could not sit in the War Department building wondering. The danger to Richmond was too great—and all other plans, to stiffen Johnston on the Chickahominy, to use Jackson in the Valley, could well seem scraps of paper if those batteries were passed. Davis, as restless as Lee, rode the eight miles to Drewry's Bluff to observe the firing. Back in the capital the shelling could be distinctly heard; and soon the names of some of the gunboats engaged were known—the *Monitor*, the *Galena*.

War Clerk Jones, affecting a calm he certainly didn't feel, waited in the same miserable suspense that Lee and Davis knew. Unless the Confederate gunners ripped their fire into gunboat portholes, any hour could see the Yankees within shelling distance of Richmond. What then? "I suppose the government would go to Lynchburg," Jones said. "I shall remain with the army and see that the tobacco be burnt." Three hours of shelling heightened the suspense; then new reports reached Richmond—heavy shot had raked the *Galena* from stem to stern, the whole Federal fleet had turned and steamed down the James!

Morale in Richmond lifted. Resolutions in Congress called on the government to defend the capital "at all hazards," and on the 20th, when Davis announced that the city would be defended, War Clerk Jones could not resist a lyrical passage:

. . . A thrill of joy electrifies every heart, a smile of triumph is on every lip. The inhabitants seem to know that their brave defenders in the field will prove invincible; and it is understood that Gen. Lee considers the city susceptible of successful defense. The ladies are in ecstasies.

Old Joe, however, was not nearly so ecstatic, nor was Davis or Lee. While the President spoke his brave words, McClellan's advance reached the Chickahominy at Bottom's Bridge and began fording the stream. For Lee, feeling with each hour of mounting pressure that his office was a cage keeping him from duty in the field, the day posed still another crisis: which way should he ask Jackson to jump? For all of Lee's gentle tact, the man's audacity—his resolution or stubbornness, as one liked—had not wavered since the first news on May 8 of Jackson's "rashness" in striking the Federals at the village of McDowell. Reading the dispatches then, Lee had glimpsed the hope that the old Calvinist had the Yankees on the run westward from Staunton.

Now, almost two weeks later, the situation had grown obscure, largely because Johnston, nearing Richmond, had wanted to exercise his authority over Jackson and Ewell. Old Joe spared none of his talent for sharpness in making this point clear to Lee. And where Johnston conceded virtue, should opportunity offer, in a joint attack by Jackson and Ewell on Banks, Johnston obviously was going to be just as happy if he found good excuse for keeping both within easy supporting distance of Fredericksburg and Richmond. Lee, for all that he was a mere headquarters general, refused to yield the belief that by smashing at Banks, Jackson and Ewell would keep McDowell's army from joining McClellan. Lee admitted his boldness—or rashness, if that was the proper word— but his instinct still urged unbalancing his opponent with speed and initiative.

Unexpectedly, withdrawing toward Front Royal, Banks confused the issue: did the Federals fear Jackson

might outflank them or were they leaving the valley to
join McDowell or McClellan? Then Banks divided his
force, one wing moving to Strasburg and another crossing the Blue Ridge toward Warrenton. Johnston's orders left Ewell no choice—he must pursue the Federals
across the Blue Ridge even if that maneuver prevented
Jackson from joining him. Thus, in effect, old Joshua
was to be left to observe Banks while Ewell moved closer
to Johnston. Lingering outside the walls of Jericho, however, had never suited Joshua's temperament; on May 20
Jackson wired Lee: "I am of the opinion that an attempt
should be made to defeat Banks, but under instructions
just received from General Johnston I do not feel at lib-
erty to make an attack. Please answer by telegraph at
once."

Lee did not flinch—next day Jackson was moving to
catch Ewell and finish the job with Banks, while Richmond (and Johnston) fended for themselves. In less
than a week Jackson was telling Richmond that "God
has blessed our arms with brilliant success," and reports
in the Northern press of Banks in frantic flight toward the
Potomac indicated that the old Calvinist had been
scrupulously accurate. Longstreet could sneer that Jackson only fought the "second raters"; a bright new star
glimmered in the Confederate heavens; and, anyhow,
Jackson could complete a half day's march before Longstreet's boys had finished breakfast.

Within twenty-four hours Jackson's triumphant dispatch was followed by evil news: McDowell had begun to extend his lines toward McClellan! [3] Official
Richmond shuddered, the city drenched in rain and
gloom. In the markets certain essential commodities were

[3] With Banks in trouble, McDowell was simply reducing his
forces so that the approaches to Washington from the Valley
could be guarded.

price-fixed to save civilians from the ravages of the ex-tortioner: a war was fought on many fronts.

Tea at ten dollars a pound or boots at thirty dollars a pair were not the apprehension that gnawed at Lee. Since May 24 McClellan had been in position on the east bank of the Chickahominy, his army reaching from Mechanicsville to Bottom's Bridge. Then two corps of Federals were thrown across the river, entrenching on a line running from Seven Pines to Fair Oaks Station. Lincoln wired McClellan on the 26th: "Can you get near enough to throw shells into the city?"—and with Federal outposts within five miles of Richmond there was strong indication that Lincoln would have his wish. Lee, watching, praying, thanked God that the heavy rain flooded the low grounds of the Chickahominy and endangered the Federal bridges.

McClellan's balloons, fastened by ropes to trees, looked down on the city. With May almost ended, Northern papers set June 15 as the outside date for the downfall of Richmond and the end of the "rebellion." On the 30th of May, with the city gray under sullen clouds following yesterday's terrific storm, Lee's taut nerves scarcely could stand the waiting. Wouldn't Johnston find something—anything—for him to do in the field? Old Joe replied vaguely, politely: and had Lee sent all the reserves he could find? Then on the 31st the Confederates struck the Federal wing at Seven Pines. By the account of General E. M. Law, who fought in Smith's division, the throwing of a Federal corps across "almost ruined bridges," the coming of darkness, and the "tardy movements of some of the Confederate commanders on the extreme right" delaying the attack several hours, "saved the left wing of McClellan's army from destruction." Law summarized Seven Pines adequately; for Lee, for the Confederacy, the day's real significance came from an entirely unexpected quarter.

Under the leaden skies that 31st of May a restless, discontented Lee rode off to Johnston's headquarters. Old Joe disagreed with Lee about the sound of firing to the southeast: no, that wasn't musketry but simply an artillery duel. Johnston rode off, leaving Lee to receive Davis, who had responded to the din of battle like a fowler after quail. Johnston had guessed wrong: he was engaged hotly and desperately, and both Davis and Lee, riding on to investigate, encountered exploding shells. The battle, surging about them, assumed a typical pattern: confused masses, musket fire poured point-blank into charging columns, a belt of woods torn to splinters by artillery, smoke hanging in low clouds everywhere, the breathless couriers, the grim litter-bearers, the screaming horses, the stench of a field hospital, the bullets chipping furrows in a tree trunk or a boy's skull . . . and then the reports that made headlines: General Wade Hampton shot through the leg, Joe Johnston wounded, perhaps mortally.

Davis and Lee watched the litter-bearers bringing Johnston up the road. Old Joe's pain from his two wounds was excrutiating; he could not stand the jostle of an ambulance. The President, Lee tried to comfort him. Then through the darkness the two men rode back to Richmond, each silent in his own thoughts, until Davis spoke suddenly: in the morning he would send Lee his orders, but the command of the army defending Richmond was his. By morning Lee was ready to rename the Army of the Peninsula.

Henceforth he would be Robert E. Lee, General, commanding the Army of Northern Virginia!

CHAPTER SIX

BEGINNING A LEGEND

FROM this moment as Lee walked forward into history
and into legend—a great figure in one and an immortal
symbol in the other—he would suffer as have few men
at the hands of biographers intent on seeing their hero
emerge full-grown like Minerva from the head of Jupiter.
The contention of Alexander Stephens that Lee was
"child-like in simplicity and unselfish in character" explained the man, but not the general. As commander of
the Army of Northern Virginia, it was Lee's shrewdness, his fast thinking, his instinct for the counterpunch,
that worked so well in his gamble on Jackson in the Valley, his ability to learn by mistake and to improvise under the pressure of necessity, that gave him dimension.
Far from springing forth neatly packaged and pre-shrunk,
in the shining armor of Minerva, it was an intensely human Lee, trusting in God that his blunders might not
prove calamitous, that somehow the Confederacy could
muddle through, who came to deserve the respect and
affection of his countrymen. It was a Lee in doubt—and
severely doubted—who took command and set a course
with such mastery that every battle he fought became
part of a single campaign.

Little of the awe and reverence with which two generations of biographers have described Lee's rise to command was shared by his subordinates. To the generals in
the field Lee was at best untested if a charitable view was
taken of his failure in western Virginia, and it remained
a large question whether in battle he could meet the
measure of Johnston. In time, to be sure, all would agree
with Sir Frederick Maurice that whereas in the field

Johnston was possibly as good as Lee, Old Joe "lacked that wider vision, that power to look calmly beyond the dangers and perils of his immediate front to the situation in the whole theatre of war, that power, in short, which takes Lee out of the ranks of the good ordinary and places him in the select band of the supreme generals."

At first critics tended to compare Johnston and his successor to the disparagement of Lee. Certainly it was in character for "Old Pete" Longstreet, with his blunt, rough, stolid, systematic nature, to wait and watch and ponder before his somewhat quarrelsome mind decided whether the army had gained or lost. Dan Hill, always sharp-tongued, always extreme in judgment, always edgy over when next his dyspepsia and a spine ailment would plague him, could swing the pendulum of his convictions one way or the other; and Gustavus Smith, the onetime street commissioner of New York City, invariably humphed and hawed and tugged at his enormous ears before relaxing the frown that came so naturally to his big, pompous face. Dick Ewell—"Old Baldhead"—squinting a pair of popeyes down a long beak, an enthusiastic amateur cook who complained almost constantly of indigestion, savored all sauces and personalities cautiously; and the other Hill—Ambrose Powell Hill, no relation to Dan—a good brigade leader despite poor health, a frail body, and previous experience limited to serving as superintendent of the United States Coast Survey, likewise would find apprehensions to mutter into his thick, auburn beard. Each liked Lee, the Virginia gentleman; each had been satisfied with Lee as the headquarters general; but Lee the commander of the Army of Northern Virginia they had yet to understand.

Lee's military brilliance rested in the fact that he never overestimated his fighting potential. On the Peninsula, for example, he must oppose 80,000 men to McClellan's 105,000, a circumstance as fixed as the necessity of cooking three days' rations before a battle. Thus from the beginning Lee realized that he was neither able to pay too high a price for his victories nor equipped to stand too long on the defensive. The Washington policy was to end the war as quickly as possible; and the Richmond policy, as Lee shaped and directed it, was to sustain the war through wit and maneuver to the point where the North grew thoroughly tired of a conflict that posed no immediate threat to its own basic way of life. His first problem was to avoid a prolonged investment of Richmond, which could only exhaust his army; and so Lee, who was actually one of the most imaginative generals in history, again relied on the swift, unexpected counter-punch.

In short, Lee dealt in realities. The fighting at Seven Pines, on the surface, had decided almost nothing. But Lee suspected that the right wing of McClellan's army, north of the Chickahominy, was "in the air," and with exact knowledge of the Federal position he saw the chance to strike a blow that would give him the initiative. In Jeb Stuart, the young lieutenant who had gone with Lee in 1859 to capture John Brown at Harper's Ferry, there was always an element of innate risk; but Lee chose now to beckon Jeb from the wings and place him on the stage of the Confederacy as one of its most romantic figures.

Stuart, not yet thirty, a cavalry leader who liked to have his banjo-player riding at his side, would be called by a Union general "the best cavalry leader ever *foaled* in North America," and the statement may have been true. With Stuart rode the Southern novelist John Esten Cooke, who believed that Jeb's "blue eyes, flashing beneath a 'piled-up' forehead, had at times the dazzling brilliancy attributed to the eyes of the eagle"; and one can accept, if one likes, the testimony of another witness that when, with the sound of a bugle, Jeb swung himself into the saddle, "his cheeks glowed and his huge mustache curled with enjoyment." Jeb was cast in the mold of a "joyous cavalier," who rode off "with his floating plume and splendid laughter," who went into "the hottest battles humming a song," who was called "frivolous" by "precise people," but who, stirring his friend Cooke to waste no cliché, "craved those perils and hardships which flush the pulses and make the heart beat fast."

Lee must have known his man, for his orders in sending Stuart's cavalry on a reconnaissance in the rear of McClellan's army asked him "to accomplish all the good you can without feeling it necessary to obtain all that might be desired." Stuart strode off with his own notions, and at two o'clock on the morning of June 12 awakened his camp with the shout: "Gentlemen, in ten minutes every man must be in the saddle!" Lee's son Rooney and sober nephew Fitzhugh were among those Jeb jerked from their slumbers. So, with a kind of gay impetuosity, began "Stuart's ride around McClellan," one of the truly unbelievable exploits of the war; and when at the close of the first day Prussian-born Heros von Borcke could record that "we continued our march, greeted everywhere with enthusiasm by the inhabitants, especially the ladies," it became understandable why Cooke believed Jeb enjoyed war "as the huntsman enjoys the chase."

Through the 13th and 14th Lee waited while a fierce, dry sun blistered the Virginia countryside—"Unionist weather," it was called—and then a courier from Stuart brought a report of what the "reconnaisance" had accomplished. One of McClellan's wagon trains had been destroyed. Federal prisoners totaled 165 or thereabouts; horses captured exceeded this number; the aggregate of Stuart's casualties: one. After circling the entire rear of

McClellan's army, Stuart had reached the Chickahominy thirty miles below Richmond. Would Lee make a diversion on the Charles City road so that the Federals wouldn't cut off Stuart on his ride back to headquarters?

Next day Stuart himself appeared before Lee, brimming with news: bad roads bedeviled the Federals behind their lines, McClellan's right was as much "in the air" as Lee suspected, and by turning Beaver Dam Creek the Confederates could sweep down on White House, whence McClellan drew supplies by wagon train and railroad. Lee's eyes sparkled. During the remainder of the war he would be hard-pressed to find a more considerate opponent than McClellan; not only had "Little Mac" graciously permitted Mrs. Lee and daughter Mary to pass through his lines to Richmond when the Federals had overrun them living on the old Custis place at White House, but now, quietly fortifying his position, McClellan apparently had decided that Lee would await his leisure for the next move.

On the 11th, loading eight regiments of Whiting's division on trains at the Richmond terminus of the Danville Railroad, Lee already had begun to prepare his surprise for the napping McClellan. Crossing the cars over the river to a point near Belle Island, where Federal prisoners were about to be released and sent down the James, the story would soon be circulated that Whiting's boys must be on their way to join Jackson in a savage thrust toward Washington. Just what McClellan's cautious nature would draw from this movement Lee could only conjecture; but surely it indicated no lack of confidence on Lee's part that he felt himself a match for McClellan and it blighted in the bud any flowering of renewed hope that McClellan could expect support from McDowell.

But Lee used Whiting's troops as a double-edged sword—"The object is to enable you to crush the forces opposed to you," Lee wrote Jackson, after which, leaving his "enfeebled troops" in the Valley, Jackson was to "sweep down between the Chickahominy and the Pamunkey" with his main army. Soon Jackson was marching and countermarching with strict orders to his boys to give but one reply to all questions: "I don't know"; and it was no surprise that Robert Stiles, seeing Jackson "stark and stiff in the saddle," should think: "If he were not a very good man, he would be a very bad one." For a time Jackson and his army seemed simply to vanish; then on the 15th he was at Ashland, fifteen miles from Richmond. Leaving his tired troops to rest, "Old Jack" pushed on to Lee's headquarters at Fair Oak Station—in the romantic phrase, "red with the dust of three Virginia counties"—and finding Lee engaged, waited quietly outside, unrecognized, a weary man who had used relays of horses to cover fifty-two miles since one o'clock that morning. Dan Hill's cadaverous, haunting eyes could not be fooled; riding up to headquarters, he spotted the travel-tarnished Joshua with eyes half-closed under the visor of his mangy cadet cap. Hill recalled:

We went together into General Lee's office. General Jackson declined refreshments, courteously tendered by General Lee, but drank a glass of milk. Soon after, Generals Longstreet and A. P. Hill came in, and General Lee, closing the door, told us that he had determined to attack the Federal right wing and had selected our four commands to execute the movement. He told us that he had sent Whiting's division to re-enforce Jackson, and that at his instance the Richmond papers had reported that large re-enforcements had been sent to Jackson "with a view to clearing out the Valley of Virginia and exposing Washington." He believed that General McClellan received the Richmond papers regularly, and he [Lee] knew of the nervous apprehension concerning Washington. He then said that he would retire to another room . . . and would leave us to arrange the details among ourselves. The main point on his mind seemed to be that the crossings of the Chickahominy should be covered by Jackson's advance down the left bank, so that the other three divisions might not suffer in making a forced passage.

During the absence of General Lee, Longstreet said to Jackson: "As you have the longest march to make, and are likely to meet opposition, you had better fix the time for the attack to begin." Jackson replied: "Daylight of the 26th." Longstreet then said: "You will encounter Federal cavalry and roads blocked by felled timber, if nothing more formidable; ought you not to give yourself more time?" When General Lee returned, he ordered A. P. Hill to cross at Meadow Hill, Longstreet at Mechanicsville Bridge, and me to follow Longstreet. The conference broke up about nightfall. . . .

Jackson rode off, apparently able to exist without sleep. Lee's love for a ruse would be revealed that night when Dan Hill's division moved toward the Mechanicsville Bridge: "To conceal the movement our campfires were freshly lighted up by a detachment after the troops had left, and a company was sent some miles down the Charles City road to send up rockets, as though signalling an advance in that direction." Lee must have been growing fond of McClellan's uninquisitive nature, if gullibility is not the word. For some reason that perhaps only the super-sleuth Allan Pinkerton could explain—Pinkerton already had galvanized McClellan with the fearful report that the Rebel force against him had now "swelled to nearly 200,000 effective men"—McClellan had the Chickahominy flowing between the two wings of his army. Thus his lines of communication ran over marshy roads and poor bridges; and since Pinkerton had his "shrewd and daring agents" knowing everything else, perhaps they understood why McClellan was based on

the Pamunkey so that his lines of communication had to
be protected by keeping his right wing between Richmond and the Pamunkey.

Lee had McClellan hung over the Chickahominy like
an ox over a fence. While the *Richmond Examiner* prepared a blistering attack upon "impatient critics" who
spoke "upon a policy, the facts of which they do not
know," Lee worked quietly. At 707 East Franklin
Street, Mrs. Lee and Mary could only gaze at the ailan-
thus trees and pray for the man they rarely saw. On the
25th the intermittent rain stopped and Richmond beheld
a rainbow. That omen to one as deeply mystical as Lee
must have seemed encouraging, and yet the hardheaded
uncertainties of impending battle remained to disturb the
long night for Lee. At three a.m. Jackson was scheduled
to advance so that he could fall on McClellan's exposed
right wing while Hill smashed at the front. Old Jack had
set the date, though Longstreet had doubted if he would
be ready. So much depended on the right timing—would
Jackson be there? With morning, Lee moved his headquarters to the Mechanicsville turnpike. The sky indicated a hot, fair day.

Climbing the hill by the Jewish Cemetery that morning of the 26th, War Clerk Jones heard the rumbling
of distant guns on the Pamunkey and cried exultantly:
"That is Jackson! He is in their rear!" When guns
sounded to the northeast, Jones shouted: "Hill—in their
front!" But Jones erred gravely. An hour later Jones, on
his hillside perch, estimated the reports of cannon at
"3,600 per hour," and thought rapturously: "This is
Lee's grand plan of battle—Jackson first, then Hill, then
Longstreet—time and distance computed with mathe-
matical precision!" Later Jones would realize the hard
lesson he was learning—war seldom worked that neatly.

For Jackson had fumbled; at daylight, already three hours later, he was just marching his men out of Ashland for Cold Harbor, filled with fulminations for Federals who had driven in his cavalry pickets and cut the telegraph; he would not contact McClellan's outposts until late afternoon. All through the morning A. P. Hill waited to start his troops forward. Then it was noon, one o'clock, two, the valuable daylight slipping away and no message from Jackson. At three o'clock Hill knew he must move or give up the day's fighting. He sent Field's brigade to take the Mechanicsville Bridge, captured it quickly, threw his whole brigade across the swamp in safety. Smartly, Field's brigade swung down the road toward Mechanicsville—withstanding a brisk Federal artillery fire, a dogged infantry contest.

Lee, however, had no reason for elation. So far Hill's men had contacted only the Federal advanced force and still needed the support of Jackson. Sooner or later McClellan intended to fight with vigor, and Lee, tormented by the risks of his first battle, could only wait and pray. A mile or so back of Mechanicsville ran Beaver Creek Dam. Here the left bank could be a Federal stronghold, peppered with artillery emplacements, lined with rows of infantry in rifle pits. Nor were all the reports from the fighting at Mechanicsville entirely encouraging. Some of the Confederate raw troops had panicked. The moment was scarcely propitious for Davis, the Secretary of War, and others to appear. Lee snapped: "Who are all this army of people, and what are they doing here?" A stunned, embarrassed Davis answered: "It is not my army, general." But Lee had no time for protocol: "It is certainly not *my* army, Mr. President, and this is no place for it." Davis said quietly: "Well, general, if I withdraw, perhaps they will follow." The President raised his

hat "in another cold salute" and found a high bank and
bushes whence he could watch the battle screened from
"Lee's repelling observation."

Lee could not mistake the vicious nature of the battle from the sounds that roared at Beaver Creek Dam.
Heavy Federal guns were pounding Hill's troops—Lee
could only listen, with a kind of mute, stomach-tight
fascination, and perhaps with a stirring of that distress he
had felt years ago at Vera Cruz when he had watched
his brother Smith under fire. Then a young army engineer, he had felt only the responsibility for the battery
he had constructed; now each boy who bled and fell and
died was *his*. There for the first time, in his mind and in
his heart, was the raw, brutal meaning of command: with
Richmond at his back, the life of the Confederacy in his
hands.

Later would come the couriers, the messages: on those
hillsides at Beaver Creek Dam the Yankee corps was
commanded by Fitz-John Porter, whom McClellan considered a fine, capable commander. The Federal guns
pounded Hill mercilessly, shot and shell blanketing the
creek before him. A frontal attack semed suicidal, but
Hill hesitated for another reason. Now—at long last
now—there should be some sound of the advancing
Jackson! At Ellison's Mill, Pender's brigade waded the
creek, forcing a passage to the right of Field's troops.
Pender reeled back, withered by the Federal fire; he tried
again, and again, and again—game and bloody and battered. A part of Dan Hill's command came up, supported Pender, drove once more at that Federal left,
which must be turned if there was to be a victory. Still
there was no progress against the blazing guns on the hillside.

Night came on. In the darkness toward eight o'clock,
toward nine, the flashes of the Federal weapons still hur-

tled defiance. Lee turned away from the scene, grim and
quiet. He knew: Confederate blood soaked the ground;
this was a repulse, savage and staggering. But war was a
fickle mistress, quick to desert one suitor for the next. This
Lee knew also. He kept his head. With the bridge to
Mechanicsville uncovered, Lee had turned to the divisions of Longstreet and Dan Hill. Now while A. P.
Hill's boys lay on the ground they had won that day, Dan
Hill marched along the Upper Cold Harbor road to
meet with Jackson. Longstreet was to bolster A. P. Hill.
The dawn, breaking over scenes strewn with the dead
and the wreckage of battle, showed McClellan the trap
Lee had sprung on him—Jackson, swinging to the east,
would flank the Federal position on Beaver Creek Dam
and make the base at White House untenable. Before
daylight the blue-clads began to pull out of the hills. Lee
soon could see columns of smoke rolling upward—the
equipment McClellan could not carry off he was burning. Repulse, and now victory, with the passing of a
single night's darkness!

McClellan's right wing, commanded by Fitz-John
Porter, fell back to a high bend on the Chickahominy
near Cold Harbor. But Lee had no idea of giving Porter
respite in covering McClellan's retreat. Watching Lee
come to his decisions, a witness thought that he was "without a shade of inequitude or irresolution." Yet the emotional range of battle is from ecstasy to black melancholy;
Lee was still to have his share of both.

Powell Hill's boys, seasoned troopers from the fight
at Mechanicsville and Beaver Creek Dam, believed with
Lee that the Federals would dig in for battle at Powhite
Creek, but again faulty maps tricked the Confederates,
not even showing a turgid stream known as Boatswain
Swamp. To the south rose a long, steeply graded hill
with the ground in the rear sloping to the flats of the

Chickahominy. Here Powell Hill's troops were engaged before Longstreet could come to their support or Jackson's flanking column protect their left. Thus exposed, the Confederate charges gained no more than a terrier's nips at the paws of a stone lion. Sweltering heat, rolling in shimmers that mixed with the bursting shrapnel—that was about the sum of it.

Yet Lee, scrapping one plan, improvised another as, stoically and steadily, Dan Hill's troops reinforced Jackson in a stubborn movement to the left. Lee's good sense took the time to set his attack. With Powell Hill still pounding furiously at the Federal center, with Dan Hill spreading around to the extreme Federal right, and, finally, with Jackson pushing into the gap between the two Hills, the troops of Old Baldhead Ewell and a portion of his own division, the afternoon had worn past five o'clock. Lee found Jackson sucking on a lemon.

Lee listened to the musketry fire, which seemed almost deafening. "Do you think your men can stand it?" he asked Jackson.

Tart and sour like the lemon, Jackson said: "They can stand almost anything! They can stand that."

It was a rotten fight for the Confederates, particularly for Powell Hill and Longstreet, who were making one bloody charge after another without a chance to maneuver or attack the flanks. But there were still the regiments of Whiting's division to throw into the battle—confident, aggressive boys led by such high-spirited combat officers as the blond, blue-eyed Texan-by-adoption John Bell Hood, at thirty an ungainly but fierce little warrior. The handsome, pugnacious "Little Billy" Whiting—no cadet at West Point ever had equaled his rating—likewise fancied himself quite a fighter. Coming up behind the remnant of Powell Hill's troops, pressing on to the crest of the ridge, breaking into a trot down the slope, Whiting's

division went with just one notion: to save the day for
Lee. It was past seven, with the sun slipping behind the
trees on the far side of the Chickahominy, as Gaines'
Mill or Cold Harbor mounted to its final full fury. Another of Whiting's brigade commanders, E. M. Law, remembered: "Men fell like leaves in the autumn wind."
But Whiting's boys were not alone; Powell Hill started
an advance, Longstreet's, Ewell's, Dan Hill's boys were
swept along, cheering and full of fight — and Northern
readers, scanning the report of the correspondent for the
New York Tribune, were stunned by the story they
read:

. . . It was an awful firing that resounded from that
smoke-clouded valley—not heavier than some in the earlier
part of the engagement, but more steady and determined . . . our officers judiciously ordered their men to
fall back . . . [but] they ran back—*broken, disordered,
routed.* . . . A motley mob started pell-mell for the
bridges. They were overtaken by many just from the woods,
and it seemed as if Bull Run were to be repeated. . . .

That scene was one not to be forgotten. Scores of rider-
less, terrified horses dashing in every direction; thick flying
bullets singing by, admonishing of danger; every minute a
man struck down; wagons and ambulances and cannon block-
ading the way; wounded men limping and groaning and
bleeding amid the throng; officers and civilians denouncing
and reasoning and entreating, and being insensibly borne
along with the mass; the sublime cannonading, the clouds of
battle-smoke, and the sun just disappearing, large and blood-
red—I can not picture it, but I can see it and always shall.

At the end such was Cold Harbor, a decisive victory
for Lee, whom John Esten Cooke would see on the field
of battle "erect and graceful . . . in the saddle, his im-
posing dignity of demeanor, and his calm and measured
tones, as deliberate as though he were in a drawing-

room." Lee told Davis that he was "profoundly grateful to Almighty God" for his success; but the devil's price still had to be reckoned with: probable Confederate dead and wounded, 8,000, against Federal losses in killed, wounded, and missing of 6,837.

Next morning one of Ewell's officers, climbing a tree, reported the Federals moving southward; and, at Lee's direction, Stuart's cavalry and Ewell's infantry cut the York River Railroad, leaving McClellan dangling without a base of supplies. Lee toured the fields of yesterday's action and, reaching the Rockbridge artillery, roused a young man sleeping under a caisson. Prodded into wakefulness by a sponge-staff, young Rob, dirty, ragged, and unkempt, blinked in embarrassment at Lee and his staff with "their fresh uniforms, bright equipments and well-groomed horses." But finding Rob safe satisfied Lee; what next to expect from McClellan was not so easily resolved. Obviously "Little Mac" had two courses to choose from: a quick race down the Peninsula, which meant the humiliation of admitting defeat; or a flight to the James and the cover of the gunboats, either to escape or to recondition his army for another assault on Richmond. Lee found it difficult to believe that McClellan was simply running.

In retrospect the next few days must have seemed somewhat nightmarish to Lee, compounded as they were of a succession of missed opportunities arising out of bizarre circumstances. The blunders that permitted McClellan to escape were largely the result of human frailty, and Lee had to assume his share of them. Again, as in western Virginia, he seemed to trust too blindly to subordinates; again the worthlessness of Confederate maps became a distinct disadvantage; and the inability of the Confederates to use artillery well was no less grim a lesson, if a newer one, for Lee to ponder.

The trouble started with Magruder, who, alerted on the 28th to report at once any Federal movement, developed a case of acute jitters; even with Confederate picket lines often less than half a mile from the invaders, it was not until the day after the Federal retreat began that Prince John seemed to understand the situation. Lee now also was convinced that McClellan was making for the James, and threw the bulk of his army across the Chickahominy in determined pursuit. At about three o'clock on the afternoon of the 29th Magruder caught up with the Federal troops in position near Savage Station; here, unsupported, the Yankees held Magruder off while McClellan's army plunged into dismal White Oak Swamp. Yet the engagement was not without its theatrical touch for Prince John, who remembered that the navy had constructed a "Railroad *Merrimac*," consisting of a thirty-two-pound rifle mounted on a freight truck and pushed by a locomotive. An eyewitness felt that the "Railroad *Merrimac*" worked well at Savage Station with "its large shells exploding right and left," but it wasted time, which was the ally that could help the Yankees most in crossing White Oak Swamp under cover of darkness.

Frustration piled upon frustration for Lee, who was hoping for nothing less than the annihilation of McClellan's army. Yet the will in Lee to destroy the great Federal columns, crowded into the swampy lands of the narrow Peninsula, burned deeply. He had baited the trap sensibly: sending Jackson down the Chickahominy, whence his infantry should be able to give quick support wherever needed; routing Hill and Longstreet along the Darbytown road, whence they were to turn left toward White Oak Swamp; putting Huger on the Charles City road, poised to snap at the retreating column at the swamp. Meanwhile he had sent Holmes to occupy Malvern Hill, backed on the James—but Holmes, deaf and incompetent, never reached his objective in the face of fire from Federal gunboats.

Sunday, June 30, was the day when Lee had to win— McClellan, crossing White Oak Swamp should be highly vulnerable. Magruder, set to the task of following doggedly after the retreating McClellan, had Lee's repeated promise of support from Jackson. That assistance would never come, for Old Jack, with hair, skin, eyes, and clothes now all the same dusty hue, was in a "peculiar mood." He had not helped Magruder, he said, because of "other important duty," and as far as anyone could judge, the old Calvinist meant that he had decided to spend Sunday as a good Christian. He was painfully slow in reaching White Oak Swamp; then, finding the Yankees had burned the one good bridge, he fell into a strange inertia when he appeared to have every chance of catching the Federals in tight quarters. Hampton found a ford that would support a pontoon bridge, but Jackson didn't seem to care. He wrote a letter to his wife, wanting her to know how much sleep he had lost and how much money he thought she should give to the church. He fell asleep in the middle of eating supper. Colonel Long (of Lee's staff) recorded that Jackson "sought a short repose," that his staff "out of mistaken regard . . . permitted him to sleep far beyond the time he had allowed himself," and that "he awoke . . . greatly chagrined at the loss of time that had occurred, the damage of which he was unable to repair." Something of Lee's "chagrin" also can be imagined when Longstreet's and Powell Hill's divisions caught up with the Federal columns at Frazier's Farm and fought fiercely until nightfall without the expected (and desperately needed) support of the lethargic Jackson. McClellan occupied Malvern Hill that night.

July 1 brought Lee a bitter decision. Yankee artillery

had been shrewdly placed, and it was not until late in the afternoon that Lee felt ready to strike the Federal left, with Magruder attacking this flank while Dan Hill threatened the center and a revived Jackson occupied the right. Confusion ruined the Confederate effort; Magruder supported too late, drifted too far to the left, pulled back into greater chaos, dented the crest momentarily but collapsed under sheer weariness: Dan Hill said afterward: "It was not war—it was murder." Jackson did very little; why, his actions indicated, try to budge a Union position that wouldn't give? The sun disappeared and rain fell heavily. Exhausted Rebels dropped down beside their arms, and supposed that they would have another crack at the bluecoats in the morning. A dense fog at daylight became a drenching rain by ten o'clock, but by then the weather made little difference: McClellan had pulled out completely, reaching the cover of his gunboats. Next day he was even safer under those gunboats at Harrison's Landing.

Not all that could be said of Lee's tactical shrewdness, under the circumstances, had reason to be complimentary. Lee had hoped to destroy the Federal army, and it remained uncomfortably intact; despite this fact, the Richmond Whig snapped that Lee's handling of the Battles of the Seven Days had "amazed and confounded" the "detractors" of Lee. War Clerk Jones felt vastly satisfied, sneering at McClellan's army: "The serpent has been killed, though its tail still exhibits some spasmodic motions." Between extremes of criticism and adulation, the objectively minded could nod at the Whig's praise of Lee's "fertility of . . . resources, his energy and daring." Here was a general—surely one worthy, as soon happened, of having a variety of tomatoes named in his honor.

CHAPTER SEVEN

INTERLUDE IN MARYLAND

NOW at last Lee found time to see his wife at 707 East Franklin Street. Poor Mary Lee, more crippled than ever with arthritis, spent almost all her time on crutches or in a wheel chair. Still she kept No. 707 a cheerful place, more given to informality than her fastidious general-husband, presiding gracefully over gatherings that came to be called "The Mess," laughing at the inflamed charges in Northern papers that the Confederates not only had hung a Zouave but also had cut him in four pieces (a persistent Northern rumor, at least as repeated in troubled Richmond, declared that the Confederates tied Federal prisoners to trees, then bayoneted them), knitting and sewing on the back veranda, or scraping lint and making bandages.

Young Rob came home on a short furlough, the result of a minor illness, and found Lee "the same loving father to us all." According to War Clerk Jones, Lee's powers had become so broad that "the Secretary of War has but little to do." A raid by Morgan into Kentucky cheered Richmond with reviving hopes that Kentucky, Tennessee, and even Missouri, would yet rise in "rebellion."

There was more than enough of a discomfiting nature in the military situation to occupy Lee. McClellan's ninety thousand poised at Harrison's Landing, remained a formidable threat, and Lee had to calculate that McClellan might cross the James and come at Richmond through the back door of Petersburg. Washington, however, was worried about its own doors, back and side; and by pooling the forces of McDowell, Banks, and Franz Sigel had gathered an army of forty-three thousand in northern Virginia to serve under one of the strangest characters Lincoln yet had found in the Union's military barrel. General John Pope bounded over the Blue Ridge greatly admiring his own achievement in breaking the Confederate hold on the upper Mississippi with his success at Island No. 10.

Filled with energy and profanity ("God damn McDowell! He is never where I want him!"), the bustling gamecock from the Midwest prepared for his glorious rendezvous with destiny. "I have come to you," prattled Pope, "from an army . . . whose policy has been attack, not defense." This truly incredible man, with his truly incredible flow of words, also said: "Let us look before and not behind. Success and glory are in the advance. Disaster and shame lurk in the rear."

But Pope specialized in surprises. On July 23 he decided to make a real mark in history with a general order that told his commanders to "arrest all disloyal and male citizens within their lines or within their reach in rear of their commands" and if those arrested refused to take the oath of allegiance they "shall be conducted south, beyond the extreme pickets of this army, and notified that if found again, anywhere within our lines, or at any point in the rear, they will be considered as spies and subjected to the extreme rigor of military law." If any of his troops were fired on by "bushwhackers," private homes would be "razed to the ground" and the "bushwhackers" would be "shot without civil process." His army was directed to live off the country and not to waste "force and energy . . . protecting private property of those most hostile to the Government." Five hostages were seized to give bite to this order, which, in the opinion of the New York World, transformed Pope's soldiers into "unbridled and unscrupulous robbers."

Lee was infuriated. Richmond accused Pope of turning the war "into a campaign of robbery and murder against unarmed citizens and peaceful tillers of the soil"; in consequence the Confederacy now was "driven to the necessity of adopting such just measures of retribution as shall seem adequate to repress and punish these barbarities"; and Pope, General Steinwehr (who had seized the five hostages), and their commissioned officers were "expressly and specifically declared to be not entitled to be considered as soldiers." In transmitting this order to Washington, Lee wrote in part:

The President also instructs me to inform you that we renounce our right of retaliation on the innocent, and will continue to treat the private enlisted soldiers of General Pope's army as prisoners of war; but if, after notice to your Government that we confine repressive measures to the punishment of commissioned officers, who are willing participants in these crimes, the savage practice threatened in the order alluded to be persisted in, we shall be reluctantly forced to the last resort of accepting the war on the terms chosen by our enemies, until the voice of an outraged humanity shall compel a respect for the recognized usages of war.

Of his nephew, Louis Marshall, Lee wrote that he could forgive his "fighting against us, but not his joining Pope." Increasingly, Pope became a thorn that festered in the flesh of Lee; with a rare flash of contemptuous humor, he called him that "miscreant Pope" who needed to be "suppressed."

Within the Army of Northern Virginia during those muggy days of July there was often more hot temper than cold reason. Bitter gossips saw Fitzhugh Lee being moved ahead in the cavalry through family influence; General Toombs believed Dan Hill had doubted his courage and wanted to meet him on the dueling ground;

Longstreet could not stand the praise going to Powell Hill and placed him under arrest; War Clerk Jones reported rumors that Magruder and Huger might be tried by court-martial; and Jackson told Congressman A. R. Boteler that Lee was "repeating the blunder we made after the battle of Manassas, in allowing the enemy leisure to recover from his defeat and ourselves to suffer by inaction," though Jackson added that his confidence in Lee was so great, "I am willing to follow him blindfolded." At times during the pursuit of McClellan, and especially in White Oak Swamp, Jackson had seemed to be trying that precise trick.

Aloof from the bickering, Lee reasoned out his next move. With Pope on the line of the Rappahannock, threatening the railroad from Richmond to Gordonsville and then a movement upon the capital, Lee determined to wriggle out of this nutcracker between McClellan's 90,000 and Pope's 43,000. At last he gave the revived Jackson his head, sending him with Ewell's division to Gordonsville. Next he rescued Powell Hill from the vindictive Longstreet by shunting him off to Jackson. Old Jack attacked part of Pope's army at Cedar Run on August 9, shied away when Federal reinforcements arrived next morning, and even if Longstreet contended that Jackson was again excelling against the second-raters, the psychological effect of Cedar Run upon jittery Washington was eminently satisfying.[1] McClellan, reducing his plea for reinforcements from 30,000 to 20,000, doggedly insisted that "it is here on the banks of the James

---

[1] In high glee War Clerk Jones recorded that General Prince was among the prisoners Jackson sent to Richmond, adding: "He affected to be ignorant of Pope's brutal orders. . . . When Prince was informed that he and the fifty or sixty others taken with him were not to be treated as prisoners of war, but as *felons*, he vented his execrations on Pope. They were sent into close confinement."

River that the fate of the Union should be decided," but on August 7 Washington ordered him to join Pope, warning somewhat sinisterly that his "reputation" might be "involved" in the rapidity with which he moved. Actually Lee had advance information of this Federal withdrawal, for on August 4 Mosby, the partisan ranger, reaching Hampton Roads in an exchange of prisoners, learned from a sympathetic steamer captain that McClellan would soon be sailing up the Chesapeake.

With McClellan hustling back to defend Washington, Lee saw his chance to whip the fretful Federals, and on the 13th Longstreet was hastened to Gordonsville with Stuart following. Six days later Lee and his staff ascended Cedar Mountain to reconnoiter the Federal position. His own army and that of Pope were placed about equidistant from Culpeper Court House, with the Confederates in position to gain the Federal rear. Still, Lee had to wait for his cavalry, and a costly wait it proved. Pope learned of his peril from a captured cavalryman; next day the Federal camps bustled, indicating a fast retreat toward the Rappahannock. So began the race against time that produced the battle of Second Manassas. Nerves in Washington fluttered with new violence at the information that Pope had recrossed the Rappahannock; troops not only from McClellan's Army of the Potomac but also from Burnside's expedition into North Carolina were reported hurrying to his aid.

Lee had not the slightest intention of giving the "miscreant Pope" any respite; Stuart was sent to turn Pope's right, gain his rear, and tear up the Orange and Alexandria Railroad. Jeb crossed the Rappahannock, a few miles above Warrentown Springs, on the 21st, slithered through mountain spurs and forests to Warrentown, and in the midst of a fearful nighttime rain smashed at Cutlett's Station on the railroad, capturing the Federal en-

campment there. (Included in the booty was Pope's let-
terbook and other valuable papers.) Stuart hadn't lost a
man; no wonder "the joyous cavalier" grew into a legend.

Lee's comment on Pope at Second Manassas was that
he "did not appear to be aware of his situation." Jackson's 20,000 reached and destroyed Manassas on the
26th, then fell back toward Sudley and later Groveton,
holding Pope more or less at arm's length until Lee could
come up. McDowell on the 27th was sensibly obstructing Thoroughfare Gap, Lee's only road of approach, so
that Jackson could be crushed before Lee joined him;
Pope, however, hoping to "bag the whole crowd"—
meaning Jackson's force, of course—next morning ordered McDowell to Manassas. So Pope set out to find
Jackson, who had disappeared; and Lee came on to attack Pope. In the eloquent statement of John Esten
Cooke, "all parties were thus moving to and fro"; the
bird's-eye view must have been ludicrous. Yet Lee at
least knew that Jackson, with his back to the mountain
beyond Groveton, waited for him; Pope, marching and
countermarching, simply couldn't find Jackson. In personal command of Longstreet's corps, Lee reached the
western end of Thoroughfare Gap about sunset on the
28th. Artillery fire toward Groveton indicated that Pope
had stumbled on Jackson. A small Federal force defended
the Gap, but Lee, reconnoitering, and, in Cooke's words,
"buried in reflection and deliberating at his leisure," finally ordered the shaggy defile stormed. Next morning
Lee was through, and Longstreet's corps fell into position on the right of Jackson.

Second Manassas often is called one of Lee's military
masterpieces, which is setting rather a high premium on
any contest with Pope. Again Lee's rule of command
that once he sent his brigade and division commanders
into battle, "I leave my duty in the hands of God" would

cost him justifiable discomfiture. At any rate, Old Pete
Longstreet was slow that day in divining what duty God
would reveal to him. Pope brought up his forces, piece-
meal, to confront Jackson; the obstinate Longstreet refused three times to respond to Lee's urging to attack.
The curious situation that resulted has been succinctly described by Sir Frederick Maurice: "On this day Jackson
had to play the part of Wellington at Waterloo, and
stand the pounding until Longstreet, in the role of Blücher, gave the *coup-de-grâce*. But the *coup* was not
given."

Many reasons can be advanced for Longstreet's extraordinary obduracy—that Lee's bloody, unnecessary
battle at Malvern Hill still haunted him, or that, as General Maurice has pointed out, "he believed the recipe for
victory to be to manœuvre an army into a position such
that the enemy should be compelled to attack at a disadvantage, and there await the blow"—but it was equally
within Longstreet's character rather to look down his nose
at Lee and to feel he was the stronger and wiser man. For
one human being to want to dominate another, even in
battle, was not a trait of men that Old Pete invented;
moreover, the longer Lee hesitated, unsure of the soundness of his own orders, the greater grew Longstreet's ob-
stinacy, but again this was predictable human behavior.

On the 29th of August, Longstreet's strong-willed
mind, obsessed with fighting one kind of war or none at
all, probably saved Pope's army from complete havoc.
The Federal forces under Porter confronting Longstreet
were inferior in number, and Old Pete, had he struck,
would have found their flank shamelessly weak. Of
course Pope, consistent to the end, understood next to
nothing of Longstreet's strength; he kept urging Porter to
attack Longstreet, but Porter held back, a more prudent
man; and so Pope cashiered Porter for refusing to fall into

the trap that Longstreet wanted to set for him. The French would have accused both Pope and Lee of failing through defects of personal qualities—Pope overaggressive, Lee too timidly the gentleman-general.

Meanwhile, what of Old Jack? Certainly on the 29th at Second Manassas the Jackson who had won out at White Oak Swamp bore magnificently the brunt of battle. "Failing to manage a fight," it was said of Jackson, "he loved next best a long Presbyterian sermon, Calvinistic to the core"—so at White Oak Swamp he worshipped and at Second Manassas he had his fight. Again Mrs. Chesnut quoted a general as saying of Jackson: "He was the true type of all great soldiers. He did not value human life where he had an object to accomplish. He could order men to their death as a matter of course." How deeply Jackson's spirit dominated the first bloody afternoon at Second Manassas would be revealed by Maxcy Gregg, the rich South Carolinian bachelor-lawyer-literary dilettante turned brigade leader rallying his troops in the heat of the third charge. "Let us die here, my men," cried Gregg, "let us die here!" Die a great many did, but Jackson, rusty and ferocious in his disreputable cadet cap, never yielded: at sunset the Yankees were reeling back in shocked retreat.

Through the night Lee reworked his plan, counting on the 20,000 reinforcements he had called from Richmond and knowing that Pope, supported by troops from McClellan, would have his full force on the field. Pope's genius for guessing wrong did not fail him now; with masterly denseness, he decided that Lee's readjustment of troops must be a Confederate retreat. At about noon on the 30th, Pope threw another Federal assault at Jackson. This time Longstreet, finding the field set to his liking, counterattacked with great spirit on the Federals' left. Pope, shaken to the core, drew reserves from his center and right to stave off Longstreet. Jackson crashed down on the weakened Federal right. Lee watched the rout, not recognizing the begrimed Confederate gunner who came up to greet him. It was young Rob. Lee smiled. Confederate battle flags pursued the disordered, retreating Yankees. "This Army today achieved on the plains of Manassas a signal victory over combined forces of Genls. McClellan and Pope," Lee wrote Davis at ten o'clock that night, and the stature of Lee no longer could be denied. Indeed, as he had promised, he had "suppressed" the "miscreant Pope" so thoroughly that he would be most distinguished through the remainder of the war for his relative obscurity. But the larger success exalted the South. Just three months before, Richmond had struggled against a queasy sense of impending disaster. Now stomachs in Washington were constricted.

It was expecting too much of human nature to believe that Lee could have his smashing victory at Second Manassas without criticism, some of it rather severe. The matter of his handling, or mishandling, Longstreet on the first day remained. Others wondered if Lee had moved faster, catching Pope between the Rapidan and the Rappahannock, it might not have been easier to destroy him, but this is playing history by second guesses, and it confounds most other forms of human futility. A sharper, more justified criticism scored Lee for not chasing and smashing Pope's disordered columns while he had them on the run; but Lee could not know that the approaches to Washington were poorly defended, and, as he afterward said, "My men had nothing to eat." A siege of Washington did not fit Lee's military temperament— here was a possible innate weakness, but it was difficult arguing with a man of success. Moreover, Lee suffered the pain of two sprained wrists, and broken bones in one hand, the result of being thrown from a frightened horse;

it would be weeks before he could write his own letters or dispatches. Reading the reports of victory at Second Manassas, War Clerk Jones said happily: "That is glory enough for a week," and Jones's was one of the many voices quelling the grumbling from the remaining "detractors" of Lee.

Yet, in a very real sense, both Lee and the Confederacy overestimated the importance of Second Manassas. True, the war now unquestionably had been prolonged, and Washington had been rocked on its political foundations, but the change had not been altogether one-sided. A weakness of the Confederacy—of Lee—was to misjudge the strength, the intelligence, the shrewdness of Lincoln, who, bringing his mind to a keen focus on Lee, became his principal adversary. It was always too easy for the South (proving that John Pope held no patent on mistaking situations) to dismiss Lincoln with a mocking shrug, to ridicule him as a rough Illinoisan who would have been ill at ease in a Richmond drawing-room, to ignore rather than to evaluate his obvious greatness as a leader. Even Lee couldn't understand how much Lincoln already had won in holding the loyalty of the border states; nor could he comprehend how, in terms of psychological warfare, slavery might yet be molded by Lincoln into a weapon of moral fission. The image of this great American conflict as the world would ultimately retain it was still evolving; the raw emotions were undefined. Lee still fought with a superb wholeness, repelling an invader from the soil of his beloved Virginia; but Lincoln, growing in confidence in his dealings with the border states, would turn in his attack on Lee by transforming this belief into a seeming sophism and pitting the South not only against the North but also against one of the basic aspirations of humanity. Even in the dark hour following failure on the Peninsula and at Second Manassas, this seed of Confederate defeat had been planted. Perhaps without Lincoln the North lacked the will to fight a prolonged war, as Lee hoped; but already Lincoln was calculating that risk and intending to meet it, and herein arose the greater struggle behind the roaring guns and glinting bayonets.

The Lincoln whom the South did not know in 1862 recoiled in despair at the news from Second Manassas. For weeks he had been drawing from the Library of Congress books on military science and trying to learn why he had no general who could use the great fighting force that the Army of the Potomac represented. Distraught and sleepless, he paced the rooms of the White House. Alone, two days after Second Manassas, he tried to understand the war anew, and he wrote for his own meditation a document that revealed Lincoln—his will, his spirit, his purpose—as few papers do. In the words that follow, a mystical Lee was pitted against a mystical Lincoln:

The will of God prevails. In great contests each party claims to act in accordance with the will of God. Both *may* be, and one *must* be wrong. God cannot be *for*, and *against* the same thing at the same time. In the present civil war it is quite possible that God's purpose is something different from the purpose of either party—and yet the human instrumentalities, working just as they do, are of the best adaptation to effect His purpose. I am almost ready to say this is probably true—that God wills this contest, and wills that it shall not end yet. By His mere quiet power, on the minds of the now contestants, He could have either *saved* or *destroyed* the Union without a human contest. Yet the contest began. And having begun He could give the final victory to either side any day. Yet the contest proceeds.

Congressional elections approached, a factor ensuring a rising tempo to the struggle. The Lincoln of 1862, unknown by the Confederacy or by Lee, badly needed a Union victory, even a partial one, to strike the smashing blow he had in mind.

The crisp, bright days of early September found Lee facing the need to move somewhere. With the Federals in the fortifications of Washington, and Richmond one hundred and fifty miles away, he must advance or retreat. His men were hungry and his horses needed forage, which made his situation unhappy in this country already blighted by two major battles. To fall back toward Richmond, protecting his lines of communication, invited the Federals to carry the war once more into northern Virginia, which was throwing away all the advantage he had won; and with sixty thousand fresh troops reported strengthening the Federal forces at Washington, Lee's army, if it lingered too long where it now stood, would soon be opposing worse odds than it had yet faced. Lee considered movements southward to Warrenton and westward into the Valley, but again these posed the possibility of bringing the war back toward Richmond. Irresistibly, the logic of the situation drew Lee's gaze toward Maryland. Why not pluck this border state for the Confederacy and then slice into Pennsylvania, giving the North a real taste of its own war? Even Old Pete Longstreet was attracted by the idea, telling Lee that in Mexico troops had subsisted on corn and green oranges, so why wouldn't the "roasting corn" of Maryland support their forces? On September 4 the Army of Northern Virginia began moving from Dranesville to Leesburg; a day later, with dusty bands playing "Maryland, My Maryland," tattered, gray-clad columns forded the Potomac.

Lee rationalized his invasion of the North, politically as well as for military reasons. Had not the Federal Government forced Maryland to stay in the Union, even suspending for a time the writ of habeas corpus? Indeed, were there not in Maryland numerous Southern sympathizers awaiting liberation so that they could join the Confederacy? On September 8 Lee issued a proclamation "To the People of Maryland," assuring them that his people had "long watched with the deepest sympathy the wrongs and outrages that have been inflicted upon the citizens of a Commonwealth allied to the states of the South by the strongest social, political and commercial ties." He spoke, Lee said, with the "profound indignation" of the Southern people, who had seen

. . . their sister state deprived of every right, and reduced to the condition of a conquered province. Under the pretense of supporting the Constitution, but in violation of its most valuable provisions, your citizens have been arrested and imprisoned upon no charge and contrary to all forms of law. The faithful and manly protest against this outrage made by the venerable and illustrious Marylanders—to whom in better days no citizen appealed for right in vain— was treated with scorn and contempt. The government of your chief city has been usurped by armed strangers; your Legislature has been dissolved by the unlawful arrest of its members; freedom of the press and of speech have been suppressed; words have been declared offences by an arbitrary desire of the Federal Executive, and citizens ordered to be tried by military commission for what they may dare to speak.[2]

[2] Maryland's Governor Thomas H. Hicks defeated strong disunionist sentiment by refusing to call the Legislature into session; at this time neither Virginia nor Lee favored secession. On April 19, 1861 a Baltimore mob fired on the 6th Massachusetts, killing four soldiers and wounding several. To a Baltimore delegation, protesting this "pollution" of Maryland's soil by Federal troops en route to Washington, Lincoln replied stiffly that "our men are not moles, and can't dig under the earth. They are not birds, and can't fly through the air. There is no way but to march across, and that they must do." On April 22, 1861 General Scott or any officer in command was authorized to suspend

Lee, continuing, believed that Marylanders "possessed a spirit too lofty to submit to such a government"; his army had come "to aid you in throwing off this foreign yoke. . . . This, citizens of Maryland, is our mission, as far as you are concerned." Neither "constraint upon your free will" nor "intimidation" would he allow. And Lee concluded:

. . . Within the limits of this army, at least, Marylanders shall once more enjoy their ancient freedom of thought and speech. We know no enemies among you, and will protect all of every opinion. It is for you to decide your destiny, freely and without restraint. This army will respect your choice, whatever it may be; and, while the Southern people will rejoice to welcome you to your natural position among them, they will only welcome you when you come of your own free will.

Lee hoped for Maryland recruits, and, quite carried away by his first adventure into diplomacy, urged Davis to propose peace—contingent, of course, on the recognition of Southern independence. He wrote to the President:

Such a proposition, coming from us at this time, could in no way be regarded as suing for peace; but, being made when it is in our power to inflict injury upon our adversary, would show conclusively to the world that our sole object is the establishment of our independence and the attainment of an honorable peace. The rejection of this offer would prove to the country that the responsibility of the continuance of war does not rest upon us, but that the party in power in the United States elect to prosecute it for purposes of their own. The proposal of peace would enable the peo-

the writ of habeas corpus, where necessity warranted, along the railroad line from Washington to Philadelphia. Lincoln, acting within legal rights, asked his critics: "Are all the laws, *but one* to go unexecuted, and the government itself go to pieces, lest that one be violated?"

ple of the United States to determine at their coming elections whether they will support those who favor the pro-
longation of the war, or those who wish to bring it to a
termination, which can be but productive of good to both
parties without affecting the honor of either.

Lee now approached the country around Frederick—
his straggling columns marching on bruised feet past fields
that promised no great abundance of food. "They were
the dirtiest men I ever saw, a most ragged, lean, and hungry set of wolves," Leighton Parks recalled in the *Century Magazine*. Struggling along in this weary, gray-clad
file, Private John Dooley, as he passed through Frederick, realized that "the large majority of the people were
silent in regard to giving demonstrations of opinion;
many because they were really hostile to us, and some
because they knew that every one was narrowly watched
by Spies, by the remnant of Yankee forces on parole in
the town, and most of all by their own neighbors." This
lukewarmness toward the Confederacy in Frederick was
part of the chilling evidence Lee gleaned that Maryland
really might not care to be liberated; although there were
some indications of sympathy, and Cooke would cite one
Marylander who fed six hundred Southern soldiers in a
single day, Lee had entered a part of the state where "entirely dissimilar to the lower counties . . . the Union
feeling was in the ascendant, as in Western Virginia." To
this disappointment Lee must add the fact that McClellan, whom he surely respected over Pope and McDowell, again commanded the Army of the Potomac as it
came out to contest his invasion. Lee's army left Frederick on the 10th and McClellan entered the town on the
13th—no world's record for a pursuit. Lee, evaluating
McClellan, confided to General John G. Walker:

"He is an able general, but a very cautious one. His
enemies among his own people think him too much so.

His army is in a very demoralized and chaotic condition, and will not be prepared for offensive operations— or he will not think it so—for three or four weeks. Before that time I hope to be on the Susquehanna."

The dash with which Lee planned his Maryland campaign stirred his generals to high spirits. Jackson he would send to Harper's Ferry, seemingly to threaten Washington but actually to capture the men and material at Harper's Ferry and to secure the Confederate line of communication from Richmond through the Valley. Meanwhile Lee intended to concentrate at Hagerstown, destroy the Baltimore and Ohio road, then march to Harrisburg, Pennsylvania. The long bridge of the Pennsylvania Railroad, crossing the Susquehanna a few miles west of Harrisburg, was to be destroyed, thus leaving the Federals no communication with the West except by the slow, circuitous route over the Great Lakes. "After that I can turn my attention to Philadelphia, Baltimore or Washington, as may seem best for our interests," Lee told a "very much astonished" Walker. But Jackson's jovial spirits, and the old Calvinist's indulgence "in a little mild pleasantry about his long neglect of his friends in 'the Valley,'" convinced Walker that this was no tale out of the *Arabian Nights;* moreover, "a party of ladies from Frederick and vicinity, [arrived] to pay their respects to Lee and Jackson."

Now occurred one of those incidents that could be accounted an act of providence or perdition, depending on whether one fought for the North or the South. Its principal actor was John M. Bloss, Company F, 27th Indiana, who approached Frederick with McClellan's advance skirmishers. Resting in the grass, Bloss spied an envelope. The two cigars it contained he divided with a comrade; then, leisurely, he began to read the paper that also fell out. "As I read," Bloss said, achieving one of the war's masterpieces of understatement, "each line became more interesting." What Bloss held was a copy of Lee's Secret Order No. 191—his complete plan for the next four days. Reputedly McClellan "gave vent to demonstrations of joy"—one scarcely wonders. Within three quarters of an hour after the discovery, orderlies and staff officers were "flying in all directions."

The date was September 13, three days after Lee's pleasant discussion of McClellan and the campaign with Walker—and, of course, the arrival of the admiring ladies from Frederick. Lee had reached Hagerstown on the 11th, expecting news next day that Jackson had captured Harper's Ferry. Twenty-four hours more passed without this anticipated news; then at two p.m. came really distressing information—McClellan on the march over the Catoctin Mountain. All at once "Little Mac" seemed to possess the instincts of a homing pigeon, threatening to isolate Lee from the three of his five detachments co-operating in the Harper's Ferry affair. Lee had not expected a fight at South Mountain, where McClellan must pass next; now Dan Hill was spurred there to contest the issue until Lee could gather his wits and rearrange his forces.

Longstreet, asked to leave one brigade at Hagerstown as a guard and speed the remainder of his command to support Dan Hill, was argumentative. Withdraw to Sharpsburg, fussed Old Pete, but Lee insisted. At nightfall Longstreet was still arguing by note that Lee should ignore South Mountain and retire to Sharpsburg; and Lee still held to his plan. The fighting next day at South Mountain was savage; Federal losses were 1,800 and Confederate casualties easily that number; at nightfall of the 14th it was obvious that unless Lee's army could be reinforced, McClellan would storm and take the mountain pass next morning. Lee lived through ten hours of dark torment—falling back on Sharpsburg after all, where his detachment under McLaws, guarding Maryland Heights for Jackson, could be brought to support Longstreet and Hill. The road was blocked with wagons; the movement became agonizingly slow. Morning saw the gray columns crossing the stone bridge over the Antietam and forming in line of battle along a range of hills between Sharpsburg and the stream. The steep banks across the Antietam seemed made for artillery, and Longstreet, riding along the ridge, snapped: "Put them all in, every gun you have, long range and short range!"

A courier dashed up to Lee. News at last from Jackson: Harper's Ferry captured with its garrison of 12,000 men, 70 pieces of artillery, 13,000 small arms!

Lee beamed at the good tidings. "Let it be announced to the troops," he said, and staff officers, galloping off, drew cheer after cheer.

"All this day," wrote William Miller Owen, a young Confederate lieutenant, "our thin line faced the whole of McClellan's army, and it closed with a little artillery practice on each side." Lee, feeling that he knew his opponent, didn't expect much fight from the cautious McClellan on the 16th, either. But Little Mac, having read Secret Order 191, felt exuberant, and reportedly was telling his staff:

"If I don't crush Lee now, you may call me whatever you please."

CHAPTER EIGHT

LOW TIDE AND HIGH

PRECARIOUS though every circumstance made Lee's position at Antietam, after his proclamation to the people of Maryland he could not slink across the Potomac without seeming a fraud. "If he had had a well-equipped army of 100,000, he could not have appeared more composed and confident," General Walker said. Instead Lee fought with a ragtag, hungry part of his army—estimates that Lee's forces had entered Maryland needing 40,000 pairs of shoes at least approximated the truth, and a North Carolinian spoke for many when he afterward wrote his wife: "People says that a man borned of woman and enlisted in Jacksons army is of a few days and short rations and i think it is nearly the same way with Longstreets."

Perched on a peninsula between the Antietam and the Potomac, with only one satisfactory ford over which to escape, with the ridges around Sharpsburg often obscuring from the left how the battle was going in the center and from the center how the fighting progressed on the right, there was suddenly a magnificence to Lee. Cheerful, energetic, unafraid, he fulfilled the Napoleonic axiom of a great general, for always he managed to remain superior to the enemy at the point of contact. Critics of Lee, who wondered if he could maneuver an army rapidly and with precision, if he could concentrate upon the threatened points in battle, studied Lee's achievements at Antietam and held their tongues. Men in the ranks saw him on Traveller, and said: "There goes Mas' Robert. . . . There goes old Uncle Robert," and the general they had followed in faith, because a soldier

couldn't argue with general orders, was now a calm, dignified, dependable man whose image had become en-
graved on their hearts.

Happily for Lee, McClellan proved almost as dila-
tory on the 16th as Lee had predicted, pushing one corps
across the sluggish Antietam so cautiously that it was
dark when Federals felt the presence of Confederates.
That day Jackson came up from Harper's Ferry—a genuinely bewildered Jackson who, knowing nothing about
the lost order, shook his head and muttered: "I thought
I knew McClellan, but this movement of his puzzles
me." Jackson told Lee that his and Walker's troops were
right behind; but at nightfall the divisions of A. P. Hill,
Dick Anderson, and Lafayette McLaws were still missing. The real fight would come next day—that was in-
evitable now—so Lee lived through another miserable
evening, praying for Hill at least to get up in time, agree-
ing that Hood's Texans were too worn out with hunger
and marching to spend the night in the front line, hearing in the black night the skirmishers pecking away at a
ghost enemy.

September 17—this "bloodiest day of the war"—
dawned, chilly and a bit damp up in those Maryland
ridges. When it ended, and the sunken road where Lee's
boys fought was renamed the "Bloody Lane," when there
were only stark memories of those who had fallen in the
bitter combat around the little white Dunkard Church or
in the cornfields and at the stone bridge, what were the
stories to tell and re-tell so that history would belong to
son as well as father, to grandson and great-grandson?

Who could forget Lee, using his thin reserves at any
point needed, stiffening the line that could not be allowed to bend, while McClellan, with overpowering
forces, held back, a mouse-like commander?

Who could forget Lee, smiling when young Rob

asked: "General, are you going to send us in again?" and answering: "Yes, my son. You all must do what you can to help drive these people back"?

Who could forget Toombs, relieved of command by Longstreet and placed under technical arrest, restored to his brigade and standing, a rock of unmovable vengeance, for over an hour on the lower Antietam?

And what of Ambrose Powell Hill—this warrior of the burning eyes whose name would be on the dying lips of Jackson and Lee—coming through the cornfield with this "Light Division," there, after the long, heated march from Harper's Ferry, at the moment when there seemed almost no time left, striking Burnside's Federals in the flank, standing up hand to hand, carrying that terrible charge—yes, what of Ambrose Powell Hill, with his bushy auburn beard falling over a red shirt?

Eight thousand Confederates lost that hot September 17, twelve thousand Yankees—this too, who could forget?

So did Antietam last through its fearful day, and through the groaning night Lee believed that the battle would be resumed on the morrow. But on the 18th the fight had gone out of McClellan, and next morning Lee began to withdraw into Virginia. He thought then, as he said later in an address to his troops, that history recorded few examples of greater fortitude and endurance than his army had exhibited. When the last of the Confederates were safely fording the Potomac, Lee was heard to say: "Thank God!"

These words also were on the lips of Abraham Lincoln. Poor excuse for a Northern victory though Antietam may have seemed, it was the best chance the man in the White House could see for striking his blow against the South. On September 22, five days after Antietam, Lincoln issued a warning that after January 1,

1863 all slaves in states still in rebellion would be declared free. The Confederacy mocked the importance of the declaration—Lincoln was trying to save his political skin and had simply gone one step farther in his conspiracy to wreck the Constitution. Angrier comment suggested raising the black flag, asking and giving no quarter.

Thus the South shrugged off the threat of the Emancipation Proclamation; there was too much of passion in the issue for the South to believe a change was coming: that not only Northerners, but people elsewhere in the world might take another view. How could this rough Illinoisan have any perceptive sense of history? Of God and morality? Yet the Lincoln who, in the bleak darkness after Second Manassas, had wondered if God's purpose in this war was different from what either party believed, tried, in the pale light after Antietam, to define, to understand. He distrusted his own judgment; he confessed the political and military considerations that motivated him; in his heart he was unconvinced that this was right.

With the leadership of the Army of the Potomac after Antietam, Lincoln had much less hesitancy. Something was deeply, radically wrong, and the search for a general who could get the most out of this fighting force—who would never let Lee escape once he had crossed the Mason and Dixon line, the sin Lincoln believed most unforgivable in a commander—became a constant worry in the White House. Finally the end for McClellan would come when Lincoln hurled at his cautious general: "I have just read your despatch about sore-tongued and fatigued horses. Will you pardon me for asking what the horses of your army have done since the Battle of Antietam that fatigues anything?" So one of McClellan's corps commanders, Ambrose E. Burnside, took over the Army of the Potomac, and Lee said sadly to Mary: "I hate to see McClellan go. He and I had grown to understand each other so well."

It was now late in October, that month when Richmond, seeing Lee for the first time in two months, was shocked at how white his beard had become. Lee "was hardly recognizable," thought War Clerk Jones. Part of the reason for the change in Lee no one understood better than Taylor, his staff aide. Not many days before, he had entered the general's tent to find Lee, overcome with grief, clutching a letter. Intelligence of his daughter Annie's serious illness had reached him just hours ago, it seemed; now, in Warren White Sulphur Springs, North Carolina, Annie was dead at the age of twenty-three. "I cannot express the anguish I feel," Lee wrote young Rob. "To know that I shall never see her again on earth, that her place in our circle, which I always hoped one day to enjoy, is forever vacant, is agonizing in the extreme." Another letter to daughter Mary cried at the same heartache: "I have always counted, if God should spare me a few days after this Civil War was ended, that I should have her with me, but year after year my hopes go out, and I must be resigned." At Lee's suggestion two lines were carved on Annie's tombstone:

> Perfect and true are all His ways
> Whom heaven adores and earth obeys.

Yet this personal anguish that traveled back with Lee on his brief visit to Richmond was little seen outside those hours alone with his invalid wife at 707 East Franklin Street; at the War Department he was calm, crisp, and businesslike, facing up to what must be expected next from the Army of the Potomac now that McClellan had been dropped in favor of Burnside. Lincoln had tried to persuade his new commander not to move too hastily against Lee, but to accumulate forces for a simultaneous assault across the Rappahannock and up the Pamunkey. The President, however, was over-ruled by Burnside, who wished to strike straight for Richmond through Fredericksburg. Lincoln had selected Burnside reluctantly, if not desperately; he appeared to be the best replacement available and almost anyone seemed better than McClellan, who had waited almost six weeks after Antietam before crossing the Potomac, then had taken nine days for that operation. Early November brought disaster for Lincoln in the congressional elections; he could not, the President growled, "bore with an auger too dull to take hold," and McClellan was relieved. The conscientious Burnside, often troubled with dysentery, assumed command of the Army of the Potomac, gravely doubting if he was up to the job. Taking a cold view of recent political reverses, Lincoln snapped: "I need success more than I need sympathy." Burnside well might fret that he was getting in over his head. Northern generals had learned by now to respect the skill of Lee.

The procrastinations of McClellan had proved no less than a godsend to Lee, for it had been a weary, tattered, straggling Army of Northern Virginia that pulled back from Maryland. If Lee's troops were low-spirited, no one need wonder: Longstreet reported more than 6,400 of his men barefoot, Jackson said he had 3,000 men without weapons, and desertions were growing serious. Foot-and-mouth disease broke out, adding to the misery of short rations, fatigue, a sense of failure. Yet Lee, always a good administrator, used the time McClellan spared him to the best advantage. He reorganized his army into two corps, under Longstreet and Jackson, and nominated both for the newly created rank of lieutenant general. Strict discipline ended the straggling; even mere strips of untanned hide fashioned into crude moccasins were better than no shoes; and Jeb Stuart in one twenty-seven-hour raid into Pennsylvania and Maryland brought back twelve hundred sorely needed horses. Soldiers not fighting often became gamblers, and many of Lee's boys turned eagerly to trying their luck at such card games as poker, twenty-one, euchre, keno, at faro and chuck-a-luck, and at the old stand-by, craps. In anger, the back of Lee's neck turned red, and games of chance, when he discovered them, did not improve his disposition. But a "revival of religion" also was reported in Lee's army, especially in Jackson's corps.

Time and rest—again, with gratitude to McClellan—healed morale. Beef and bread were not so bad—especially, as Private John Dooley remarked, "if we may get some extras now and then from home or the sutler's tent." Virginians had grown a bit hardened to what war had done to their country—"The fences are burned [Dooley saw], the meadows trampled down, the cattle all gone and the harvests unharvested; proud homesteads in ruins, the masters on the war trail and the old couple and daughters sit mournful and comfortless around expiring embers." But Dooley knew that Lee shared his sorrow and his determination to repel the invader. Sometimes Dooley felt choked at the sight of "Uncle Robert," with "his hair and beard turning grey; his mildly beaming face, large black eyes recognizing all around him; his mouth firmly but pleasantly set, and his whole figure expressing gentleness, dignity and command." When the boys in the ranks cheered, Lee answered "with a placid smile and with a dignified but most courteous bend of his head."

When during those early days of a raw, blustery November, Burnside replaced McClellan, the Federals were massed at Warrenton and Lee was at Culpeper. Jackson was back in the Valley, and Lee, who in nominating

Old Jack for lieutenant general had extolled him as "true, honest and brave" with "a single eye to the good of the service," granted him the right to act as his "discretion" dictated. Longstreet was at Culpeper. That a change in Federal command probably involved a change in the style of planning had not escaped Lee. Nor was Burnside a dallier like McClellan; soon he began his movements toward the Rappahannock, and by mid-November the two combatants moved irresistibly toward the next great dueling ground.

On November 20 a rain lashed the limbs of the oaks and maples, almost bare and gaunt now, as Lee rode into Fredericksburg. Across the river in the rolling hills of Stafford Heights he could see the Federal encampments. Next day, in a whipping storm, Lee made his first troop placements when an ultimatum came to the mayor from Burnside—either the town must surrender by five p.m. or a bombardment would start at nine on the morning of the 22nd. Reluctantly Lee advised the defenseless people to vacate their homes and gained a day's reprieve from the Yankees.

Confederate hearts tightened and Confederate tempers flared at the scene that followed. Still the storm raged. Over roads part frozen, part mud, the exodus of Fredericksburg began—women and children and the aged, silent and mournful, on foot or in weathered carriages (those with means fled southward by train), some hugging infants in their arms, most hungry, yet hardly any complaining. Watching the weary travelers, Lee retained a memory that he afterward expressed: "History presents no instance of a people exhibiting a purer and more unselfish patriotism or a higher spirit of fortitude. . . . They cheerfully incurred great hardships and privations, and surrendered their homes and property to destruction rather than yield them into the hands of the

enemies of their country." Heartsick, officers and privates
alike swore at the shame of the thing. Later they saw a
few creeping back through the rain into Fredericksburg,
for there really was nowhere else for them to live.

The Federals held off the bombardment of the town.
Lee frowned. What now? Was Burnside pulling a trick
threat while he sneaked southward to the James? Jackson
was called back toward Winchester, for another pitched
battle to defend Richmond could be in the making. The
days crept by with Burnside curiously, worrisomely quiet.
On the 29th snow began to fall and Lee drew a deep
breath. All along, he had hoped to stall off another Federal offensive until winter intervened and fighting on a
major scale became impracticable. But Confederate spies
destroyed this wish. The Federals were only waiting for
their pontoons to arrive; then they were coming across the
Rappahannock. In a depressed mood, Lee wrote to his
wife in Richmond: "I tremble for my country when I
hear of confidence expressed in me. I know too well my
weakness, and that our only hope is in God." Outwardly
he remained calm and cheerful. He had never lacked the
heart to command. Also the memory of the evacuation of
Fredericksburg ate into him, stiffened his resentment,
taunted him with its injustice. "Women, girls, children,
trudging through the mud and bivouacking in the open
fields," he wrote Mary, the grim image fixed in his mind.
Then it was December—the 1st, the 5th, the 8th, 9th,
10th—and still Burnside had not moved.

Haze partly obscured the moon at two o'clock on the
morning of December 11 when Confederate pickets spotted the first pontoniers. At four thirty that morning on
Marye's Heights, behind Fredericksburg, two cannon
roared the signal, for by then there no longer could be
any doubt that Burnside was in earnest. Down in town
General William Barksdale and his Mississippi volun-

teers waited patiently, through the fog that at dawn made it hard to see a hundred yards. Virginians told Mississippians that a lot of ground haze had to be expected this time of year when the moon was nearing the last quarter. After Second Manassas and Antietam, Virginians had grown fond of Barksdale and his boys—an easygoing lot in camp, hellcats in a battle, and it was the damnedest thing how in a fight the Rebel yell of a Mississippian sounded different from a Virginian's.

Lee also had acquired an affection for Barksdale's brigade, and that morning, standing on an eminence afterward known as Lee's Hill, he watched with satisfaction the Mississippians contesting the passage of the Federal pontoniers at the foot of Hawk Street and below the railroad bridge. Here Lee, to spare the town, could not use his artillery and had to depend on the infantry; farther down the river, near Deep Run, where Burnside attempted a third crossing, the big guns could dispute the issue. Soon the smoke from Barksdale's muskets, mixing with the fog, closed off the view from Lee's Hill. But the reports that reached the general were encouraging. The Federals would get their bridge across at Deep Run, but at Hawk Street and the railroad trestle those Mississippians were putting down a fire that had the Yankees dropping their tools and ducking.

At ten o'clock the haze lifted, the break for which Burnside had been waiting. Now on Stafford Heights the Federal artillery unlimbered—a hundred guns, fifty rounds to each, belching explosive death into Fredericksburg, rocking buildings into masses of crumbling walls, revealing behind their flaming nozzles blue-clad columns ready to cross, while over the rolling clouds of smoke two Federal observation balloons drifted placidly. The back of Lee's neck reddened. "These people delight to destroy the weak and those who can make no defense," he cried.

"It just suits them!" Later Mary would hear how the bombardment set fire to numerous houses and knocked down nearly all the homes along the river. Suddenly the guns sputtered out; the pontoniers swarmed back to the river; and so too did Barksdale's Mississippians, who had holed up through the barrage and now were madder than wet hens. But the Yankees also had their stubborn streak; finally in bateaux infantrymen fought their way across, deployed, screened the bridge-builders, and at nightfall Burnside held, for what they were worth to him, the ruins of Fredericksburg.

There was ground haze next morning that really did not drift away until noon. By then two gray-clad figures, with a guide, could be seen creeping along a ditch to a hill not more than four hundred yards from the Federals. There, behind two old gateposts, Lee and Jackson watched. Marching columns of Yankees coming over the pontoon bridges, sheeted wagons, rumbling caissons— Burnside meant to advance all right. Lee put down his glasses. He and Jackson crept back along the ditch. Lee wrote his wife that Burnside occupied the town: "We hold the hills commanding it, and hope we shall be able to damage him yet." Lee guessed that Burnside would strike at his right flank, and knew how weak it was. That night a soldier died of exposure in the cold, biting wind. Yet no picket could risk the comfort of a fire.

Jackson looked unnatural next morning. Stiff-jawed at the needling that greeted his new uniform coat and braided hat, Jackson grumbled that this had been Jeb Stuart's work, fussing and coaxing until there hadn't been any other way to please him. Old Pete Longstreet's sense of fun always cut on its sharp edge, and now, motioning toward the Federals, he asked: "Jackson, what are you going to do with all those people over there?" "Give them the bayonet," retorted Jackson. His new clothes unsettled him; also, he hated to stand on the defensive, and, with Stuart's support, had urged Lee to attack Burnside under the cover of the fog. But Lee had shaken his head. Let the Federals meet him where he stood. These were mean hills to assault. He would hold back his strength until he could make it count. Jackson had sworn he would follow Lee blindfolded, and had meant it—even in this uniform that looked dressy enough for a parade. Toward ten o'clock the sun began burning through the haze.

For Jackson it was a morning that began in strange pageantry. The sun glinted on Federal bayonets; the ground was clean under freshly fallen snow. Union officers stepped before their troops, unfolded papers, read the orders for the day. Bright battle flags whipped in the breeze. The Federals advanced in three tight lines of battle. Federal horse artillery and heavy fieldpieces boomed, rocked back on their carriages, boomed again. Quickly the north bank of the Rappahannock flamed with guns while steadily, doggedly, the blue-clad lines came on, nearing the railroad. Jackson struck back viciously, from right and right center, using deadly small-arm fire. Gaps opened in the lines. On the Federal left—at right angles to the advance—Jackson's artillery raked the enemy. The fight stiffened. Yankees gained the river road, crossed the railroad, charged the slopes where Jackson's corps stood. Thrown back to the railroad embankment, the Union forces charged again, finding a gap between the brigades of Archer and Thomas.

Jackson faced real peril. The left of Archer's brigade, believing they were surrounded, broke in utter confusion. On the right, said J. H. Moore, Confederate officers and men "were enraged at what seemed to be cowardice [they had seen the Federals thrown back on their own front] and, rushing toward the broken lines, leveled their

pistols . . . and fired into these fleeing comrades."
Somehow Colonel Turney managed to re-form Archer's
shattered lines, then fell when a Minié ball entered his
mouth and came out at his neck. The Federals emerged
from the woods, officers yelling: "Into line! Into line!"
Jackson looked licked.

But Old Jack knew the game of war—next best to
his Bible. He had held Jubal Early's division in reserve.
Now he threw those troops forward, and Archer's men
were taunted: "Here comes old Jubal! Let old Jubal
straighten that fence! Jubal's boys are always getting Hill
out of trouble!" Confederate artillery and small arms began hitting the Federals hard, jolting their cockiness,
turning them back once more to the shelter of the railroad embankment. Jackson's clothes were not so trim,
but the blue eyes were brighter.

Before the 13th of December ended, Lee, turning to
Longstreet, said: "It is well that war is so terrible—we
should grow too fond of it!" This was the day when
Burnside, thrown back on the Confederate right, soaked
the impregnable slopes of Marye's Heights with Union
blood. Earlier that morning E. P. Alexander, Longstreet's engineer and superintendent of artillery, told him:
"General, we cover that ground now so well that we will
comb it as with a fine-tooth comb. A chicken could not
live on the field when we open on it!" But Burnside was
willing to try—and more than once.

Up on Marye's Heights, behind a stone wall, Longstreet had placed T. R. R. Cobb's brigade, a portion of
Kershaw's—in all, about 2,500 men. About noon, in
order to help Jackson on the right, Longstreet ordered his
batteries to open fire wherever troops could be seen
around the city. Longstreet found quickly that this fire
"began at once to develop the work in hand for myself,"
and Burnside acted just as Old Pete wanted: "The Fed-

eral troops swarmed out of the city like bees out of a
hive, coming in double-quick march and filling the edge
of the field in front of Cobb." Down there was a sunken
road beneath a retaining wall four feet deep. A worse
height to assault could not be imagined, and yet, Longstreet remembered, "The field was literally packed with
Federals from the vast number of troops that had been
massed in the town." Then:

. . . From the moment of their appearance began the
most fearful carnage. With our artillery from the front,
right and left tearing through their ranks, the Federals
pressed forward with almost invincible determination, maintaining their steady step and closing up their broken ranks.
Thus resolutely they marched upon the stone fence behind
which quietly waited the Confederate brigade of General
Cobb. As they came within reach . . . a storm of lead
was poured into their advancing ranks and they were swept
from the field like chaff before the wind. A cloud of smoke
shut out the scene for a moment, and, rising, revealed the
shattered fragments recoiling from their gallant but hopeless
charge. The artillery still plowed through their retreating
ranks and searched the places of concealment into which the
troops had plunged. A vast number went pell-mell into an
old railroad cut to escape fire from the right and front. A battery on Lee's Hill saw this and turned its fire into the entire
length of the cut, and the shells began to pour down upon
the Federals with the most frightful destruction. They found
their position of refuge more uncomfortable than the field of
the assault.

One thrust up the slope of Marye's Heights had
hardly ended in bleeding agony when the second began.
Cobb waited quietly. It was awful what must happen:
then Cobb's guns opened, and Federal dead piled upon
Federal dead. Unbelievably a third blue wave came on,
grim, white-faced boys, brave as Trojans, coming up

through the choking battle smoke, hampered by the heaps
of their own dead, over which they must now climb,
eyes leveled at the stone wall—and again Cobb's guns
cut them down, just killing boys who had been ordered
needlessly to die. This wasn't an assault; it was a death
march. Still Lee worried. To Longstreet, who stood beside him on Lee's Hill, he wondered if the Federals
might not break the Confederate line through sheer per-
sistence.

Stoically Old Pete answered: "General, if you put
every man now on the other side of the Potomac on that
field to approach me over the same line, and give me
plenty of ammunition, I will kill them all before they
reach my line. Look at your right—you are in some danger there—but not on my line."

On the fourth charge a single Yankee came within a
hundred yards of the stone fence. There for a moment he
rose above the dead, vibrantly alive, a symbol of gigantic
heroism; then Cobb's guns mowed him down, and the
few others struggling up behind him. With a prudence a
bit excessive under the circumstances, Longstreet called
up the remainder of Kershaw's brigade, but actually Cobb
needed only the ammunition they brought—the extra
men were in the way. A fifth and sixth Federal charge
followed—to Longstreet the blue-clad boys fell "like
the steady dripping of rain from the eaves of a house"—
and then, mercifully, God closed the night over the
shameful slaughter at Marye's Heights.

A Federal straggler, captured that night, carried a
memorandum of Burnside's plans to renew the battle on
the morrow. Rifle pits were dug on top of Marye's
Heights. But the 14th and 15th brought no further fighting to disturb the dead rotting on the hillside. On the
16th Lee wrote to his wife in Richmond: "I had supposed they were just preparing for battle, and was sav-

ing our men for the conflict. . . . This morning they
were all safe on the north side of the Rappahannock.
They went as they came—in the night." Months passed
before the staggering cost of Fredericksburg to the Yankees was known—12,653 casualties against 5,309 Confederates. On Marye's Heights the Federal loss was
9,000. Of course Lee suffered sharp criticism—he had
allowed Burnside's army to escape, when, in the opinion of the London *Times*, it had been within his power
to crush Burnside "horse, foot and dragoons." All Lee
could say in reply was that he had expected Burnside to
attack again, and he hadn't; to Jeb Stuart he could add
privately: "No one knows how *brittle* an army is."
Burnside had taken risks and been massacred; if Lee had
been overcautious, he still had an army in wonderful
fighting trim. Suddenly, too, Confederate bonds were
demanding a better price.

Lee spent his second Christmas in camp, away from
his family. He commenced "this holy day" by writing to
Mary: "But what a cruel thing is war: to separate and
destroy families and friends, and mar the present joys and
happiness God has granted us in the world; to fill our
hearts with hatred instead of love for our neighbours, and
to devastate the beautiful face of this world! I pray that,
on this day when only peace and good-will are preached
to mankind, better thoughts may fill the hearts of our enemies and turn them to peace." To his youngest daughter, Mildred, he wrote that he had just seen Rob at the
head of his brigade on his way up the Rappahannock,
and added: "I am, however, happy in the knowledge
that General Burnside and army will not eat their promised Christmas dinner in Richmond today." To his
"Precious Little Agnes," Lee wrote: "I can only hold
oral communication with your sister [Mary, in King
George County, within enemy lines], and have forbid-

den the scouts to bring any writing, and have taken back
some that I had given them for her. If caught, it would
compromise them. They only convey messages. I learn
in that way she is well."

Lee's letters, that second Christmas in camp, disclosed
the hidden bruises of war on his spirit. The memory of
the evacuation of Fredericksburg was still an "acute
grief" and almost in awe he told Agnes: "The faces of
old and young were wreathed with smiles, and glowed
with happiness at their sacrifices for the good of their
country." Could so much heroism go unregarded? He
told Mrs. Lee: "My heart is filled with gratitude to Almighty God for His unspeakable mercies with which He
has granted us from the beginning of life, and particularly
for those He has vouchsafed us during the past year.
What should have become of us without His crowning
help and protection?" His army was in good health, and
he believed his soldiers shared his disappointment that
Burnside had not renewed the battle. "Had I divined
that was to have been his only effort, he would have had
more of it," he wrote. Clearly, he could be stung by
criticism. To young Mildred, away at school in North
Carolina, he sent fatherly advice: "You must study hard,
gain knowledge, and learn your duty to God and neigh-
bour: that is the great object of life."

A duty as executor of his father-in-law's will now faced
Lee, for the time had come when Custis had stipulated
his slaves should be freed. From camp Lee instructed that
those in Richmond could find employment there if they
chose; those in the country could stay on the farms or
come to Richmond. "I hope they will do well and be-
have themselves," Lee wrote. "All that choose can leave
the State before the war closes." He did not mind "the
attacks of the Northern papers" and felt it unwise to pub-
lish any reply. Businesslike, he continued:

. . . If all the names of the people at Arlington and on the Pamunkey are not embraced in this deed I have executed, I should like a supplementary deed drawn up, containing all those omitted. They are entitled to their freedom and I wish to give it to them. Those that have been carried away, I hope are free and happy; I cannot get their papers to them, and they do not require them. I will give them if they ever call for them. It will be useless to ask their restitution to manumit them. . . .

In Washington, as the New Year approached, gossips wondered. Would Lincoln stand by his promise? Would there be an Emancipation Proclamation?

CHAPTER NINE

OVER THE RIVER

ON New Year's Day 1863, Burnside called at the White House. The troubled commander of the Army of the Potomac believed that he should try again to cross the Rappahannock; his fellow generals dissented. Not even Napoleon, Lincoln said afterward, could get any good out of an army while such a spirit prevailed. Then, tired from a day of shaking hands with visitors and worried that his signature might not appear firm, the President signed the Emancipation Proclamation.

In mid-sentence, in the emerging history of the great American conflict, Lincoln placed a semicolon; the struggle that hitherto had been waged to save the national government he now enlarged to embrace a conflict as old as the memory of man—the war for human freedom. The contradiction that had been achieved could not be immediately grasped, either North or South; but where Lee was winning the battles, Lincoln was winning the campaign behind the guns and the tragic dead. This victory would be reflected first in faraway Manchester, England, where the workingmen, hard hit by the shutting off of Southern cotton, hailed an act which destroyed "the ascendancy of politicians who not merely maintained Negro slavery, but desired to extend and root it more firmly." In warmhearted reply Lincoln acknowledged "the sufferings which the workingmen at Manchester and in all Europe are called to endure in this crisis"; in supporting the Proclamation, they performed "an instance of sublime Christian heroism which has not been surpassed in any age or in any country."

The Richmond reaction was violent anger. Davis, de-

livering his annual message to Congress, suggested that
captured Federal officers now be dealt with according to
the laws "for the punishment of criminals engaged in exciting servile insurrection," and he ridiculed "this monstrous pretension" whereby neutral Europe had remained
passive "when the United States with a naval force in-
sufficient to blockade effectively the coast of a single
state proclaimed a paper blockade." Much as Davis
might like to cast all Union officers in the image of old
John Brown, he voiced an empty threat that his own
armies would not have supported. And for all the elo-
quence with which Davis reproached the neutrality of
England and France, he had lost the sympathy of the
people if not their governments; his constitutional arguments they had never understood and so they could con-
cede that he had some point, but the moral issue seemed
crystal clear.

The Confederacy, at the beginning of 1863, was feeling the sucking pull of an undertow. Longing eyes in
Richmond looked at the Copperhead movement spreading into Ohio, Indiana, Illinois, Wisconsin, and Iowa
(and claiming particular strength along the Ohio River),
and Richmond voices spoke hopefully of counterrevolu-
tion in the West. Always the pattern of Confederate apprehension was the same: salvation must surely come,
either from Europe or from the border states; the struggle was not so lonely, so forsaken as it appeared. Yet the
terrible reality remained: in the resources for waging war,
the Southern potential steadily deteriorated. At the same
time its military needs grew on three fronts: Lee pitted
against Burnside in Virginia, Bragg against Rosecrans in
Tennessee, Pemberton against Grant in Mississippi.

Before Fredericksburg, Lee could not ignore the crisis. Food to feed his army had to come from somewhere.
Blighted northern Virginia couldn't supply it. The beef

cattle that came from Richmond were so thin that Lee decided he must wait till spring and try to fatten them. Colonel L. B. Northrop, the commissary general, sitting stiff in the newspapers he wrapped around his chest in place of flannel, didn't like Lee (he didn't like anyone), and tension developed. Lee was in Richmond, conferring on the miserable beef cattle, when a Federal raid upon New Berne on January 17 frightened the eastern sector of North Carolina and stimulated a new fear that a Federal thrust from the south might be imminent. Lee agreed to detach two brigades for service in North Carolina, and then on the 18th Burnside moved.

Lee hastened back to Fredericksburg. Longstreet and Jackson bickered, neither able to agree on how to meet Burnside's threatened attack. Both might have saved their tempers, for Burnside was embarking on his hopeless "Mud March," waiting two days for a pounding rain to stop and then struggling for another two days over roads turned into sticky bogs. What little taste Burnside retained for commanding the Army of the Potomac melted away entirely. On the 25th Lincoln acceded to Burnside's request that he be relieved.

In the five weeks before Burnside floundered in the mud, Lee's training as an engineer had made the line on the Rappahannock one of the best fortified of the war. He could feel reasonably secure, and yet the pressures upon him were many. Problems of staff reorganization, of a redistribution of artillery units, of a serious shortage of horses, loaded his desk with correspondence. There developed moments of petulance, and when on one occasion his aide likewise grew huffy, Lee said: "Colonel Taylor, when I lose my temper, don't let it make you angry." He kept warning Richmond that "the enemy will make every effort to crush us between now and June," but usually the actions of Congress caused the "little nervous twist or jerk of the neck and head" that disclosed his rising temper.

Lee could not restrain his umbrage at the lawmakers in Richmond: "I cannot get even regular promotions made to fill vacancies in regiments, while Congress seems to be laboring to pass laws to get easy places for some favorites or constituents, or get others out of the service. I shall feel very much obliged if they will pass a law relieving me from all duty and legislating some one in my place, better able to do it." His resentment deepened. "What," he asked, "has our Congress done to meet the exigency, I may say *extremity*, in which we are placed?" His own bitter conviction was that Congress had "concocted bills to excuse a certain class of men from service, and to transfer another class in service, out of service, where they hope never to do service."

Lee could not stay angry very long, and, his temper spent, Colonel Taylor remembered, he "always manifested a marked degree of affability, as if desirous of obliterating all recollection of the unpleasant episode." He liked to joke, and could even smile at such standard camp humor as one soldier calling to another: "Come out of them boots! I know you're in thar—see your arms sticking out!" He liked to tease, and his conversation at meals was kept on the easy basis of talk among equals. He was known to invite his staff officers in for a drink—buttermilk, of course. "I used to think," Colonel Taylor has said, for what the opinion may be worth, "that General Lee would have been better off if he had taken a little stimulant."

For all the tedium, the hardship, the short rations that winter produced, the morale of Lee's army remained high. Again there were reports of religious revivals; but at the same time a chuck-a-luck game flourished for weeks at a gambling den called the "Devil's Half-Acre." Amateur theatricals helped to relieve the monotony, and an all-male burlesque drew from one observer the comment that though "they ware dresses" there was "not much of the Lady." Punishments in camp included "bucking," "gagging," and the "barrel shirt," which was what its name implied—a soldier forced to march in a barrel.

Private Dooley described "bucking" as a punishment where the culprit was made to "sit in a doubled up posture, clasping his knees with his hands, and whilst his knees almost touch his chin a long stick is inserted between his arms and underneath his knee joints"; in "gagging" a bayonet was placed in the culprit's mouth and held there by a cord tied behind the head. Slack discipline and Richmond bawdyhouses had taken a toll in gonorrhea and syphilis from the Army of Northern Virginia in late '62, and the Richmond *Examiner* had inveighed against "the treacherous shoals of vice and passion which encounters the soldier at the corner of every street, lane, and alley of the city"; under Lee's administration, the army became as clean as any in the war. If drunkenness was little reported, part of the answer may have been the fact that apple brandy was selling at sixteen dollars a quart. Private Dooley painted a picture of life at Fredericksburg:

By night fall we are again in bivouac making good fires, for the night is cold and our feet must be dried before we sleep. Then thousands of fires gleam out from the woods and even hillside, along the roads and deep within forest glen, and sounds of mirth and song and jest rudely burst upon the wonted stillness of solitude until the weary soldiers stretch their limbs before burning embers and dream of the "pleasant fields traversed so oft."

Lee's next antagonist as commander of the Army of the Potomac was Joseph E. Hooker—boastful, pleasure-loving "Fighting Joe," whose sharp tongue had not spared Burnside. Again, Lincoln felt forced to a reluctant choice, for Hooker was a heavy drinker and there was a real question whether he could " 'keep tavern' for a large army." But Lincoln reassured his secretaries hopefully: "He can fight"; and doubtless the President never heard, as C. F. Adams, Jr., testified that "during the winter when Hooker was in command . . . the Headquarters of the Army was a . . . combination of bar-room and brothel."

Lee's grievance with Hooker was for his tactics and not his personal habits. On February 6, admitting that with the snow, rain, and mud "I am so cross now that I am not worth seeing anywhere," Lee wrote to his daughter Agnes: "I have no news. General Hooker is obliged to do something. I do not know what it will be. He is playing the Chinese game, trying what frightening will do. He runs out his guns, starts his wagons and troops up and down the river, and creates an excitement generally. Our men look on in wonder, give a cheer, and all again subsides *in statu quo ante bellum*." Hooker became the sort of annoyance to Lee that Jackson was to Dick Ewell when Old Jack would allow no pepper on his food, swearing that it weakened his left leg. Some people were beyond comprehension.

Late February brought a foot of snow, and stretching rations to satisfy men and horses became a serious matter. "Our enemies have their troubles too," Lee wrote to his wife. "They are very strong immediately in front, but have withdrawn their troops above and below us back toward Aquia Creek. I owe Mr. F. J. Hooker no thanks for keeping me here. He ought to have made up his mind long ago what to do." Next day, in a somewhat more cheerful mood, Lee added: "The cars have arrived and brought me a young French officer, full of vivacity, and ardent for service with me. I think the appearance of things will cool him. If they do not, the night will, for he brought no blankets."

Before spring arrived, scurvy broke out, and soldiers searched the woods for the first sassafras buds and wild onions. Lee had deeper worries: in order to watch the Federals south of Richmond—and, pointedly, to help in collecting supplies, especially bacon, in North Carolina —he had detached two divisions under Longstreet. Renewed Federal activity broke out around Newport News in late March, and then a throat and heart illness confined Lee to bed for several days, where, he declared, the doctors were "tapping me all over like an old steam boiler before condemning it." It was well into April before Lee felt well again, but even then rheumatism bothered him. Federal balloons drifted above Stafford Heights, a constant reminder that Federal eyes looked down on Fredericksburg—calculating risks, Lee's weaknesses. In Tennessee, in Mississippi, spring found blue-clad columns moving against gray; Lee, asked by Richmond if he could release troops to help in Tennessee, thought that if Hooker assumed the defensive, "the readiest method" for taking pressure off Tennessee "would be for this army to cross into Maryland." He asked for pontoons to be ready to seize the offensive. Longstreet still had not brought home the bacon from North Carolina. Reports reaching Lee placed Hooker's strength between 150,000 and 160,000 effectives (the correct figure was 138,378); Lee's force at Fredericksburg, including cavalry in the Valley, could not have much exceeded 62,000. He was back where he had been at Antietam— outnumbered at least two to one, his army divided.

On April 23 a raid on Port Royal indicated that Hooker had some bedevilment in mind—his cavalry was concentrating on the upper Rappahannock and troops were coming up from the rear. Men and horses in the Army of Northern Virginia critically needed provisions, and Lee must wait for Longstreet to complete his mission to the south; if Hooker would wait until Old Pete returned, Lee said, "he will find it very difficult to reach his destination," but what if Hooker didn't wait? Lee faced the gloomy prospect: *he* would find it very difficult, even standing on the defensive, to act "as vigorously as circumstances may require."

On the 29th, about dawn, a courier from Jackson awakened Lee. Hooker was throwing his pontoons across the Rappahannock. Lee nodded. He had heard firing earlier and thought it was time "some of you young fellows were coming to tell me what it was all about." He had a message for Jackson: "Tell him I am sure he knows what to do. I will meet him at the front very soon." This confidence in Old Jack had deepened in Lee with Second Manassas, Harper's Ferry and Antietam, Fredericksburg. Jackson was like a right arm, a general he could trust to understand an idea and carry out the details on his own initiative. Through the winter the respect between Lee and Jackson had blossomed into positive affection—no one on the staff could deny that. Old Jack, grudging in praise of anyone except God, said openly of Lee: "He is cautious; he ought to be. But he is not slow. Lee is a phenomenon." Lee knew that he could fluster Old Jack by whispering he had found a little girl who wished to kiss him; but riding off through the fog that morning he could predict with equal assurance that other quality in Jackson, his steadfastness when the odds seemed hopeless.

Through the next two days the Confederates lay in their lines, trying to judge what was Hooker's real game. Lincoln had been to see Hooker and had looked through field glasses at Lee's troops around Fredericksburg. The

visit had claimed a deeper significance than sight-seeing;
could the country sustain still another bad defeat for the
Army of the Potomac? Lincoln wanted Hooker to forget Richmond—his real objective was destroying the
army in front of him. "Our communications are shorter
and safer than are those of the enemy," Lincoln wrote
Hooker, emphasizing his position. "For this reason, we
can, with equal powers fret him more than he can us. I
do not think that by raids towards Washington he can
derange the Army of the Potomac at all. He has no distant operations which can call any of the Army of the Potomac away; we have such operations which may call
him away, at least in part. While he remains intact, I do
not think we should take the disadvantage of attacking
him in his entrenchments; but we should continually har-
ass and menace him, so that he shall have no leisure,
nor safety in sending away detachments. If he weakens
himself, then pitch into him."

So did Lincoln, self-tutored in military science, prod
Hooker; with the Virginia dogwood all in bloom, blue-
clad columns began to deploy, until on the 29th it became clear that the main Federal force was concentrating
above Fredericksburg around Chancellorsville and the
Wilderness. Hooker had acted with strategical shrewdness, threatening Lee's flank; Hooker, in a gay mood,
boasted that Lee's boys "may as well pack up their hav-
ersacks and make for Richmond, and I shall be after
them." Lee did not deny the gravity of his situation, giving him a choice either to retreat to the south or to divide
again his already divided army, leaving the small force
to hold his position at Fredericksburg while with some
50,000 effectives he plunged after Hooker. Lee debated
his choice until the morning of May 1; then detailing
10,000 men to remain with Early, he marched toward
the Wilderness.

Lee knew the hard, forbidding country in which he must fight; Hooker did not. But Chancellorsville—one residence and outhouses—stood on the main road through the Wilderness from Orange Court House to Fredericksburg. It was a desolate region of owls, whip-poorwills and moccasins, of "melancholy masses of stunted and gnarled oak" where little sun could be seen, where "thicket, undergrowth and jungle stretch for miles, impenetrable and untouched"—a region where a battle seemed impossible. A contemporary account said:

. . . Into this jungle . . . General Hooker pene-trated. It was the wolf in his den, ready to tear anyone who approached. . . . Neither side could see its antagonist. Artillery could not move; cavalry could not operate; the very infantry had to flatten their bodies to glide between the stunted trees. That an army . . . should have chosen that spot to fight . . . and not only chosen it but made it a hundred times more impenetrable by felling trees, erecting breastworks, disposing artillery *en masse* to sweep every road and bridle path which led to Chancellorsville—this fact seemed incredible.

At sunset that 1st of May, Lee and Jackson moved back to a pine thicket to escape Federal sharpshooters trying to pick off gunners at a Confederate battery. Seated on a log, the two talked over the situation. Jackson thought that Hooker wouldn't really fight here, but would withdraw on the morrow across the Rappahan-nock. Lee couldn't believe that; Hooker had his main army poised to fight. They had one chance as Lee saw their position: to swing around the left flank and get into Hooker's rear. Stuart rode up with a report that the Federal right, extending west beyond Chancellorsville, was "in the air." It could be turned if it could be reached. Reconnaissance that night revealed the Federal front too strong to assault; if Hooker's exposed right wing was to be turned, Lee must support the movement by an attack from the west to turn the strong Federal positions around Chancellorsville. Was Jackson ready to go after that right wing, deep in the Wilderness? "My troops will move at four o'clock," Old Jack said. Lacy, a chaplain in Jackson's corps who once had supplied a church in the neighborhood, had tramped the roads through this part of the Wilderness and felt that horses and men could manage them.

Jackson was awake first; Colonel Long found him, shivering in the darkness. Later, warmed by a cup of coffee, he studied the maps and quizzed Lacy, fixing the roads in his mind. It was nearly daylight when Lee asked: "What do you propose to make this movement with?"

"With my whole corps," Jackson answered.

Stunned, Lee searched the ground, looked up, murmured: "What will you leave me?"

"The divisions of Anderson and McLaws."

Less than 20,000 men, Lee thought, against the 50,-000 Hooker could hurl upon him. Then, calmly, Lee said: "Well, go on."

At seven o'clock Jackson's column started along the narrow road into the sunless forest. Close behind the first regiments rode Jackson, stiff-jawed and scowling astride his horse. Lee watched Jackson ride over a crest, then turned away, remembering the somber eyes, the cadet cap.

The Federals were quiet that morning as Lee, waiting to hear from Jackson, spread out his thin line as best he could—in places his men were six feet apart—and sent a special message to Early to be sure to hold his position in front of Fredericksburg. Ten o'clock brought the sound of artillery fire westward on the road through the Wilderness; at eleven the fire grew heavier. Lee prayed that Jackson was all right, but the courier who arrived around noon brought grim news. The enemy was attacking the wagon train that followed Jackson's column!

Lee rushed forward a brigade to the threatened point. Jackson, however, had kept on, stoically, shaking free his wagons—more than ever, the gray-clad Joshua of the Confederacy. The enemy still remained quiet—proof that Old Jack's movement had not alarmed them—and then "near 3 p.m." Jackson scrawled a message to Lee. He was around—far around, about two miles from Chancellorsville—on the Federal flank and hoped "as soon as practicable" to attack. "I trust that an ever kind Providence will bless us with great success," wrote the old Calvinist, the scent of blood in his nostrils.

The wait then was harder for Lee—a straining of ears for the sound of firing that meant Jackson was engaged. Press forward at the first sure sound, Lee ordered—give Hooker no chance to detach troops to throw against Jackson. The sun started to slip away. Word came that Early, through a confusion in orders, had withdrawn from Fredericksburg, abandoning the heights to the enemy, marching to join Lee. Go back if you can, Lee appealed to Early, don't leave Fredericksburg exposed. Then . . .

Across the Wilderness came the rumble, rising in its tempo, shaking the thickets, awakening the sluggish streams where the moccasins lurked—Jackson's guns! Lee threw his thin line forward—up past the pickets and across the road, playing his bluff grandly. The 6th Virginia brought him back the colors of the 107th Ohio, a precious souvenir of their brief penetration of the Yankee's works. From dusky twilight into darkness, the Rebel yell taunted the enemy. The moon came up. Westward flashed the exploding shells from Jackson's guns—all hell appeared to have opened up over there.

Indeed, it had. Wolburn, Jackson's signal officer, rode pantingly to Lee's headquarters with the story. A mile above Wilderness Church, Old Jack had caught the Yankees flat-footed—arms stacked, cooking supper. Rebel bugles had blared, Rebel yells screamed through the woods: it had been a panic and flight, a mile to Wilderness Church, a mile beyond before darkness. Then, Wolburn said, Jackson had ridden ahead, when he had been fired on by his own men and wounded three times in the arm. . . .

Lee stared at the speaker. Wolburn tried to continue the story. Under heavy fire Jackson had been carried back to a surgeon. His pain was severe.

Tears stung Lee's eyes. "Don't talk about it," he cried. "Thank God it is no worse!"

Later a topographical engineer tried to tell Lee about Jackson and was cut short: "I know all about it and do not wish to hear any more."

Cutting open the sleeve of Jackson's coat revealed the ugly mass of blood that the general's arm had become and foretold the still uglier prospect: there was no hope of saving Jackson except by an amputation. This fact Lee did not know as he worked through the night on preparations to smash Hooker completely. A. P. Hill, who had succeeded Jackson in command, had himself been wounded; now Rodes, a brigadier general, held command until Jeb Stuart could reach the field. It was well past three o'clock in the morning when Lee dictated a message to Jeb: "It is all important that you continue pressing to the right, turning, if possible, all the fortified points, in order that we can unite both wings of the army. Keep the troops well together, and press on . . . so as to drive him from Chancellorsville, which will again unite us." He would do everything "on this side," Lee said, to accomplish the same object, and warned once

more: "Try and keep the troops provisioned and together and proceed vigorously."

Stuart struck before sunrise. He had seized Hazel
Grove, a knoll about two thousand yards from Chancellorsville, and there massed thirty fieldpieces. With this
supporting fire power, Jeb hurled his Rebels against the
Federals, yelling: "Remember Jackson—remember Jackson!" The troops charged headlong, caught up by Jeb's
spirit, hearing him sing out in taunting defiance: "Old
Joe Hooker, will you come out of the Wilderness!" Or
was it myth that Stuart burst into song? Boy or soldier—
that contradiction was difficult to resolve in Jeb.

Within moments the struggle for Chancellorsville
turned into a raging battle. Slowly, grimly, irresistibly
the lines of Lee and Stuart fought to join in the determination to drive Hooker back upon the river. Under the
furious impact of the Rebel charge, a sullen Yankee officer was telling Hooker: "I cannot make soldiers or ammunition!" Jackson's surprise attack the night before had
demoralized the Yankees—none more so than Hooker.
He watched the morning attack from the porch of the
Chancellor House, leaning against a pillar; a Confederate round shot struck the place, turning over the pillar
and hurling the Union commander to the ground. That
he had been so stunned he was incapable for the next
several hours of directing operations intelligently, no one
disputed. Yet the early exhaustion of artillery ammunition, the absence of all but one brigade of cavalry, were
mistakes Hooker could not charge to the lucky shot that
felled him.

Lee—and the ebullient Stuart—asked simply for a
little luck. It seemed incredible that against Hooker's
overpowering numbers Lee's wing should meet with Stuart's, that the Federal front should give way, that disordered blue-clads should huddle back in misery and con-

fusion upon Chancellorsville, while Southerners pursued them with yells, stormed their earthworks, swept them pell-mell out of the Wilderness. Yet John Esten Cooke claimed to have witnessed it all, and remembered:

A scene of singular horror ensued. The Chancellorsville House, which had been set on fire by shell, was seen to spout flame from every window, and the adjoining woods had in like manner caught fire and were heard roaring over the dead and wounded of both sides alike. The thicket had become a scene of the cruellest of all agonies for the unfortunate unable to extricate themselves. . . . Fire, smoke, blood, confused yells and dying groans mingled to form the dark picture.

Lee had ridden to the front of his line, following up the enemy, and as he passed before the troops they greeted him with one prolonged, unbroken cheer in which those wounded and lying upon the ground united. In that cheer spoke the fierce joy of men whom the hard combat had turned into bloodhounds, arousing all the ferocious instincts of the human soul. Lee sat on his horse, motionless, near the Chancellorsville House, his face and figure lit up by the glare of the burning woods, and gave his first attention, even at this exciting moment, to the unfortunates of both sides, wounded and in danger of being burned to death. . . .

There a courier reached Lee from Jackson, conscious after his amputation (though he gave Lee no inkling of the operation). Old Jack wanted Lee to know he had won a great victory—that to an old soldier, Lee was a general who had the virtue that counted above all others: he won. Lee choked up with emotion. Jackson, Jackson, he thought—could there be another man like him? "Could I have directed events," Lee dictated from the warmth of his heart, "I would have chosen for the good of the country to be disabled in your stead. I congratulate you upon the victory, which is due to your skill and energy."

Yet the Yankee had not exhausted his sting—nor was the victory complete. On the evening of May 2, twenty thousand Federals crossed the river and advanced on the skeleton force at Fredericksburg. Next morning two assaults carried Marye's Heights; as one angry Reb remarked, "I reckon now the people of the Southern Confederacy are satisfied that Barksdale's brigade and Washington Artillery can't whip the whole damned Yankee army!" The Union forces pressed doggedly, at sunrise of the 4th, along the plank road toward Chancellorsville; but "Brother William," the chaplain of the 17th Mississippi who had been the hero of the religious revival during the winter months, broke away on horseback to carry to Lee word of the disaster that had smitten Fredericksburg. Lee started McLaws and his division to help the beleaguered Early; at Salem Church, McLaws and Early handled the Federal threat under Union Major Sedgwick, fulfilling Lee's dry promise to Brother William: "The major is a nice gentleman; I don't think he would hurt us very badly." On May 5 Hooker was recrossing the Rappahannock, and when word of the Federal debacle at Chancellorsville reached the White House, an agonized Lincoln cried: "My God! My God! What will the country say? What *will* the country say?"

On May 7 the fearful news could not be kept from Lee—Jackson was developing symptoms of pneumonia. Lee refused to believe that Jackson might die—that God would let him die—and he told the courier to give Jackson "my affectionate regards, and tell him to make haste and get well, and to come back to me as soon as he can. He has lost his left arm, but I have lost my right." Jackson seemed to rally, but next day the pneumonia was filling the old warrior's lungs, and he lapsed into delirium. Jackson, in the shadows of his mind, went on fighting—"Tell Major Hawks to send forward provisions for the men."

In the twilight hours of Saturday, May 8, the doctors watching Jackson shook their heads. Perhaps Lee had begun to sense the truth—that Jackson was storming into the Dark Valley on his greatest campaign—but alone that night Lee prayed, admitting to God his desperate need for the man, his deep love. Jackson . . . Jackson, who would use no pepper, who blushed when little girls wanted to kiss him . . . Jackson, stouthearted, riding off into the Wilderness . . . Lee prayed and next day sent Jackson a message: "When a suitable occasion offers, give him my love, and tell him that I wrestled in prayer for him last night, as I never prayed, I believe, for myself."

On Sunday Jackson remained delirious. Dry, feverish, the lips beneath his beard moved: "A. P. Hill, prepare for action." Those straining to hear caught other words: "I must find out . . . whether there is high ground . . . between Chancellorsville and the river." Behind the closed eyes guns must have flashed, cannon roared. Jackson murmured: "Push up the columns . . . hasten the columns. . . ."

It was the end, surely the end, but Lee shook his head. "God will not take him from us, now that we need him so much," he said. Their prayers must be answered: "Surely he will be spared to us."

Jackson slept restlessly, awoke, and next day there seemed no battle behind the dimmed eyes. His voice was low, but again he saw somewhere ahead a vision . . . a promise . . . and, falteringly, the words took form:

"Let us pass over the river, and rest under the shade of the trees."

Then the old warrior quieted. He was across the Dark Valley.

CHAPTER TEN
GETTYSBURG

NEXT day Lee announced Jackson's death to the army.
"The daring, skill and energy of this great and good soldier, by the decree of an All Wise Providence, are now
lost to us," his order said. "But while we mourn his
death we feel that his spirit still lives and will inspire
the whole army with his indomitable courage and un-
shaken confidence in God as our hope and strength."
Critics of Lee insisted on giving Jackson credit for the
flanking movement that had brought the brilliant victory
at Chancellorsville; but the claim was not true. In later
years Lee wrote the editor of the *Southern Review*:
"There is no question as to who was responsible for the
operations of the Confederates or to whom any failure
would have been charged." At the moment Lee was neither interested in speculations over what might have been
nor in Hooker's efforts to minimize his defeat. Such con-
cepts and deceptions belonged to the leisure of future
historians; Lee, the general in the field, had to live with
the pressures and the obscurities of the present.

At Chancellorsville, in killed, wounded, and missing,
Hooker's losses were 16,845 and Lee's 13,156. Judging by the relative strength of the armies, Lee had suffered the greater loss, and for a government hard pressed
to support all its fighting fronts this factor was serious.
But there were other problems, none more pressing than
replacing Jackson. Lee changed the organization of his
army from two corps to three. Longstreet, of course, retained command of one; Ambrose Powell Hill, who had
been a heroic figure in his red shirt at Antietam, headed a
second; and to the dyspeptic amateur cook, Dick Ewell,

learning to manage a wooden leg, went the third. But reorganization of command could not solve the other urgency that had plagued Lee all through the winter. "It is very difficult," wrote Henry Heth, of Hill's new corps, "for anyone not connected with the Army of Northern Virginia to understand how straitened we were for supplies of all kinds, especially food."

Lee knew: the pinch was enormous. And an idea, once fixed in Lee's mind, was not easily shaken. Fighting McClellan on the Peninsula, he had believed the best way to defend Richmond was to get as far away from Richmond as possible. What choice had he, if he now remained on the defensive against an enemy "too far apart . . . to fall upon them in detail," except ultimately to retire to Richmond and stand a siege? His thoughts fell into a natural sequence: he wanted the offensive, he needed food that war-torn Virginia could not yield, and soon in Pennsylvania the young green stalks of corn would stand straight and firm. Lee's plan for a second invasion of the North was already evolving when in mid-May he was summoned to Richmond.

Again, there was the same problem with which to contend—this dumpy little fellow Grant, chewing on his cigars and making the situation at Vicksburg anything but comfortable. Lee met with the Cabinet. Should troops be detached to help the embattled Pemberton in Mississippi or should Lee invade Pennsylvania? Postmaster General Reagen alone hedged; on the 18th, Lee was back at headquarters, thinking of that fine Northern corn. Longstreet opposed the idea, believing they should help Bragg against Rosecrans in Tennessee, which was adding another element to the Confederate headache. Lee let Old Pete talk himself out: twice Lee had divided his army, and had had enough of that.

Early June found Lee and his army gathered around

Culpeper. On the plain near Brandy Station, Stuart insisted that Lee inspect a grand review of the cavalry. "It was a splendid sight," Lee wrote Mary. "Stuart was in all his glory. Your sons [Rooney and Rob] and nephews look well and flourishing." A trainload of girls had come to Culpeper for a dance, and war suddenly had become gay and lighthearted. Then in the cool dawn haze of June 9, Federal cavalry slipped across the Rappahannock and gave Stuart one of the nastiest fights of his career. After several hours the bluecoats were thrown back, but Stuart had not explained why he had not known of the presence of the Federals or why that blunder had justified 523 Confederate casualties. The Richmond *Examiner* snapped: "If the war was a tournament, invented and supported for the pleasure of a few vain and weakheaded officers, these disasters might be dismissed with compassion." Such criticisms, suddenly plentiful, seared Jeb's pride; the war in succeeding weeks would turn on that fact.

After the battle Lee faced a sad, personal duty, writing Mary that he had seen their Rooney carried, wounded, from the field. "He is young and healthy, and I trust will soon be up again," his letter said. He decided that Rob should take Rooney to Hickory Hill, a residence about twenty miles from Richmond. To Rooney's wife, Lee did not deny his grief. But he continued hopefully: "As some good is always mixed with the evil in this world, you will now have him with you for a time, and I shall look to you to cure him soon and send him back to me."

Lee tried to forget his concern over Rooney as he prepared to move north. With gray-clad columns starting toward the Potomac and over the Blue Ridge, Lee reverted to the role of diplomatist. Yet now, in writing to Davis, he could not disguise pessimistic undertones: "We

should not . . . conceal from ourselves that our resources in men are constantly diminishing, and the disproportion in this respect between us and our enemies, if
they continued united in their efforts to subjugate us, is
steadily augmenting." How could they avoid this ultimate calamity? He came to the heart of his letter—came
to it blindly, no more informed in '63 than he had been
in '61 or '62 over why the North supported Lincoln,
reading with wishful eyes newspaper accounts about
Copperheads and Peace Democrats (who in another
year would be making his old antagonist McClellan
their Presidential candidate)—missing at every point
any insight into political know-how or the home-front
psychology of war. Lee wrote:

Nor do I think we should, in this connection, make nice
distinctions between those who declare for peace uncondi-
tionally and those who advocate it as a means of restoring
the Union, however much we may prefer the former.

We should bear in mind that the friends of peace at the
North must make concessions to the earnest desire that exists
in the minds of their countrymen for a restoration of the Union, and that to hold out such an inducement is essential to
the success of their party.

Should the belief that peace will bring back the Union
become general, the war would no longer be supported, and
that, after all, is what we are interested in bringing about.
When peace is proposed to us, it will be time enough to
discuss its terms, and it is not the part of prudence to spurn
the proposition in advance, merely because those who wish
to make it believe, or affect to believe, that it will result in
bringing us back to the Union. We entertain no such apprehensions, nor doubt that the desire of our people for a distinct and independent national existence will prove as stead-
fast under the influence of peaceful measures as it has shown
itself in the midst of war. . . .

Perhaps the British—a Gladstone or Russell or Palmerston—trained to eccentricity, could have seen something useful in Lee's proposals; for Davis, who must deal in American realities, the suggestion of laying down arms on one basis to discuss peace on another, and then whipping up the will to fight again if these negotiations fell through, could only be excused if motivated by utter guilelessness. Happily, Lee soon was hustling on to fight the war, at which, indeed, he remained the most adept man in the Confederacy.

Ewell, stomping around on his peg leg, led the Second Corps across the Potomac under orders to collect horses, cattle, and flour, and "if Harrisburg comes within your reach, capture it." Longstreet followed Ewell. A. P. Hill had the job of watching the Army of the Potomac, and, if necessary, of keeping it occupied while the First and Second Corps moved into Pennsylvania. Hill fussed, not so much over the Yankees as over his wife, who kept lingering on a visit to headquarters. Finally by mid-June both Mrs. Hill and the Federals moved—one home, the other to make a stand between Lee and Washington—and Hill hastened to join the other corps. "It's like a hole full of blubber to a Greenlander," cried Ewell, viewing the abundant Pennsylvania countryside. Dorsey Pender of Hill's Corps wrote his wife: "We might get to Philadelphia, without a fight, I believe, if we should desire to go"—precisely what many Northerners feared, for on the 27th a proclamation began with the ominous words: "Citizens of Philadelphia: Prepare to defend your homes."

On the 15th Governor Curtin gave Pennsylvania official word of the invasion, and a kind of dread and resignation spread over the state. Then on the 28th Lincoln played his old trick with the Army of the Potomac, jug-

gling the high command and replacing Hooker with
George Gordon Meade, West Point-trained and Penn-
sylvania-born. As a boy Meade had played with Mc-
Clellan and with that turncoat Philadelphian, Pemberton, whom Grant had holed up inside Vicksburg. In the
army Meade was known as a humorless, conscientious,
hard-working fellow, not given to "reviews" like Burnside or to "sociability" in the sense applied to Hooker. He
was a listener rather than a talker; his mind seemed com-
prehensive; all in all, the army had been led by worse.
Meade was headquartered at Taneytown and Lee at
Cashtown. Neither had the least intention of fighting a
battle at the drowsy little town of Gettysburg, about mid-
way between them.

If Lee knew much less than he should about the
strength and position of the Federals, the reason behind
that unhappy circumstance was a rider on a horse who,
fording the river at three o'clock on the morning of the
27th, sat wet and dripping on the shore of Maryland.
Still stinging from the rebukes that had followed the
cavalry skirmish near Brandy Station, Stuart had screened
the movements of Hill and Longstreet. Lee's next orders had directed Stuart to join Ewell, and obviously
speed had been essential to Lee, who, in hostile country,
required close touch with "the eyes" of his army.

Jeb was resting at Rockville that day when one of his
boys spied a Federal train of 150 wagons coming down
the road from Washington. Jeb couldn't resist tempta-
tion—here was a prize that would arouse Southern im-
aginations and recapture his prestige. The spirit of the
foray was caught by W. W. Blackford, who rode with
Stuart: "After them we flew, popping away with our pistols at such drivers as did not pull up. . . . It was as
exciting as a fox chase for several miles, until when the
last was taken I found myself on a hill in full view of

Washington." No one doubted Jeb's immense glee, or
that Sweeney, the banjo-player, was set to strumming
"The Dew is on the Blossom" and "My Wife's in Cas-
tle Thunder." This exploit, and time spent tearing up
the B. and O., had only one bad feature: at Cashtown
Lee's army was blind without its eyes.

Confederate General Henry Heth traveled to Gettysburg with five brigades in the early morning haze of
July 1. His object: to get shoes for the barefooted men in
Hill's Corps. It was a sleepy-eyed lot who swung along
the Chambersburg Pike toward a stream known as Willoughby Run. Suddenly instinct warned Heth—a cover
of woods, the declivity of the stream. He was right: the
Federals were there, he had a fight on his hands, and,
in the phrase newspaper reporters loved so dearly, "the
ball was opened" at Gettysburg.

At Cashtown Lee heard the sound of battle. A spy had
brought word that "a pretty tidy bunch of blue-bellies
[were] in or near Gettysburg," and Lee, spurring Traveller along the pike, expected the report Heth gave him.
"The enemy had now been felt and found to be heavy in
force," Heth later wrote, laconic to the point of decep-
tion, for the Yankees had handled him roughly—General
Archer captured, two regiments of Joe Davis's brigade
surrendered. When Heth re-formed his battered brigades at Willoughby Run, the battle hinged on how
quickly Ewell, marching the Second Corps from Fay-
etteville to Cashtown, could whirl his columns around.

What Lee was to see that afternoon, looking down
upon Gettysburg, was the Federal army split. Hill, gathering strength, smashed the Yankees at Willoughby Run;
and Robert Rodes, who for a time had commanded for
the fallen Jackson at Chancellorsville, engaged two Yankee divisions along Seminary Ridge. In an old railroad
cut came the climax for Rodes. Down there smoke-

blackened Federal cannoneers, the water in their buckets like ink, were chanting: "Feed it to 'em, God damn 'em, feed it to 'em!" But one Rebel line came up when the first melted away, and the Yankees began falling back down the railroad track, turning and firing as they retreated. It was, the Rebs said, a "brisk little scurry."

Some claimed that the Federal retreat through Gettysburg was orderly, others that the Yankees broke and ran like frightened rabbits; but, in either case, Sallie Broadhead, Gettysburg schoolteacher, knew that "the town was full of filthy Rebels." Ewell, who led the Confederate pursuit, rode into town, mingling with his exuberant soldiers, refusing a bottle of wine pilfered from a cellar, ignoring younger officers who insisted they should keep after the Yankees before the enemy entrenched in the heights beyond the town. Ewell was through for the day, a man obviously feeling the strain of his artificial leg and depressed in mind. Lee, seeing the enemy retreating and telling his adjutant general it was necessary "only to press those people in order to secure possession of Cemetery Heights," fell into his old weakness of trusting his lieutenants too much. That night exhausted Federals lay beside the tombstones, gaining the day by forfeit. A Louisiana captain groaned: "Our Corps commander was simply waiting orders, when every moment of time could not be balanced with gold."

Longstreet, who had never wanted to fight in Pennsylvania, joined Lee about five o'clock that afternoon. Old Pete liked nothing about the situation—Gettysburg, with the Federals occupying the heights, was Marye's Heights in reverse.

"If the enemy is there tomorrow, we must attack him," Lee said.

Longstreet snorted. "If he is there," he said, "it will be because he is anxious that we should attack him."

Was there a better reason for getting out? Moving around
Meade's left, Lee could put the army between Meade
and Washington, threatening his left and rear and forcing him to fight wherever they chose to meet him.
Meade's army, not its position, was Lee's objective.

At Second Manassas Old Pete had managed to bend
Lee, but since then that trick had become increasingly
difficult. Lee wanted to fight, despite Longstreet's insistence that with Pickett's division still coming from
Chambersburg and Stuart out of reach he would be exposed in detail. "He seemed under a subdued excitement,
which occasionally took possession of him when 'the hunt
was up,' and threatened his superb equipoise," Longstreet recorded. "The sharp battle fought by Hill and
Ewell on that day had given him a taste of victory." A
troubled Longstreet parted with Lee.

July 2 brought overcast skies, sultry heat, a mizzling
effort at rain. Through the night the Federals had entrenched on Cemetery Ridge; now through the morning nothing happened beyond the pecking-away of
skirmishers and sharpshooters. At five o'clock that morning Colonel Freemantle of Her Majesty's Coldstream
Guards, an observer with the Army of Northern Virginia who liked to sit in trees and watch battles, had
found Lee and Hill whittling sticks as they discussed
the day's plan. Lee was anxious to mount an early assault, later telling Hood: "The enemy is here, and if we
do not whip him, he will whip us." Hood carried this
message to Longstreet, who was fretful over how much
the Federals could see of his movements from their signal station on an eminence known as Round Top, and
Hood remembered that Old Pete replied: "The General is a little nervous this morning; he wishes me to attack; I do not wish to do so without Pickett. I never
like to go into battle with one boot off." The events of

the day would substantiate Hood's memory—Old Pete waited all through the morning, and then into the afternoon, for his other boot.

Lee squirmed. At two o'clock he told Freemantle hopefully that if he wanted a good view of the battle he had better return to his tree, but, Freemantle said, "until four-thirty p.m. all was profoundly still," and it began to look doubtful "whether a fight was coming off today at all." Then Longstreet, still without his boot, deployed and his cannon opened. Spiritedly the Federal artillery replied. In the still air dense smoke rose along the six-mile front—"the air seemed full of shells," caissons blew up, across the field Yankee yell hooted in defiance at Rebel yell. Colonel Freemantle looked down from his perch:

So soon as the firing began, General Lee joined Hill just below our tree, and he remained there nearly all the time looking through his field glasses—sometimes talking to Hill and sometimes to Colonel Long of his staff. But generally he sat alone on the stump of a tree . . . during the whole time the firing continued he only sent one message and only received one report. . . . When the cannonade was at its height, a Confederate band of music, between the cemetery and ourselves, began to play polkas and waltzes, which sounded very curious accompanied by the hissing and bursting of shells.

The artillery tapered off. Now Longstreet had the battle he didn't want—"the best three hours of fighting by any troops on any battle field," he said of this day when American history would write into its pages unforgettable, homely names: Little Round Top, Big Round Top, Devil's Den, the Peach Orchard, the Wheatfield. Lee's strategy had Longstreet striking the right flank and Ewell the left, with Hill holding the cen-

ter and preventing quick Federal deployment of reinforcements to any sector that weakened.

For the millions of Americans who have visited Gettysburg, this fighting on the second day—perhaps Longstreet's greatest day—is better known than any in history: how at almost the last moment the Federals reinforced and held the Round Tops, towering, rock-strewn
slopes that were the key to the Federal position; how the
furious impact of Longstreet's charge through the Peach
Orchard and Wheatfield ripped the Union's Third
Corps to shreds and kept alive the hope that this driving
Confederate wedge could split the Army of the Potomac; and how, as the shadows lengthened, with the
Rebels within fifty yards of the Federals' works, Meade,
with eyes tired, red and worried, rallied his Yankees and
broke the dogged advance. Then only the still field remained with the wounded and dying, the cedar canteen
of the Rebel beside the tin canteen of the Yankee, the
broken wheels, the limber-boxes, the dismantled guns,
the discarded knapsacks. Soon would come the ambulance corps, working through the night by twinkling
lanterns. Meanwhile Colonel Freemantle could climb
down from his tree.

Lee, leaving his stump, received no visit from Longstreet that evening, but simply an oral report: either
Old Pete was overly fatigued or still sulking. Around
the other end of the Federals' U-shaped line at Culp's
Hill, Ewell's boys clung as night came on, holding a
section of the enemy's front trenches. Some of Hood's
Texans still held a toehold along the western slope of
Little Round Top, and Longstreet ruled the Peach Orchard. Lee had three prongs of the Confederate fork in
Meade's hide: would it be enough, with another jab
tomorrow, to unseat the Federal giant on the ridges and

open up the road to Baltimore and Philadelphia? Good
artillery positions had been wrested, the fighting morale
of the Army of Northern Virginia remained high, and
now Pickett's division was coming up . . . Lee, still
full of fight, thus justified his resolution to stand pat for
another tiff with Meade.

In later years Longstreet would say of July 3, 1863
that he was never "so depressed as upon that day." His
dispute with Lee continued, bitterer at rock bottom, for
to Old Pete it was more imperative than ever to move
around Meade's army. Lee said simply, looking across
the 1,400 yards separating the two forces, Longstreet's
whole First Corps must make the assault.

Old Pete said snappishly: "It is my opinion that no
15,000 men ever arrayed for battle can take that position!" But Lee was inflexible. A bombardment would
clear the way. Colonel Freemantle could not resist re-
cording Old Pete's extraordinary behavior thereafter:
"At noon all Longstreet's dispositions were made; his
troops for attack were deployed into line and lying down
in the woods; his batteries were ready to open. The general then dismounted and *went to sleep* for a short time."

Over at Culp's Hill there was bad news for Lee.
Ewell simply couldn't do anything right—losing the
heights through hesitation the first day, attacking with
too little and too late the second, and this morning jumping the timing of his assault so that it did not fit with
Lee's revised plan. Ewell gave the Federals a stiff fight
for Culp's Hill; by ten o'clock assault and counter-assault
were swift and murderous, with the dead and wounded
piling up in windrows—it was "lovely fighting along
the whole line"—but by eleven o'clock Ewell was
beaten.

Lee did not lose heart. Overhead a blistering sun beat
down. Men dozed. Pickett's boys, moving up, pelted

one another with green apples. Lee nodded and the cannon roared—roared as never guns roared at Second Manassas, at Antietam, at Fredericksburg, at Chancellorsville, roared as perhaps never before on the American continent (save a few days before under Grant at Vicksburg) had cannon roared—stunning on Cemetery Ridge Yankees like Frank Haskell:

. . . We see the solid shot strike axle, or pole, or wheel, and the tough iron and heart of oak snap and fly like straws. The great oaks there by Woodruff's guns heave down their massive branches with a crash, as if the lightning smote them. The shells swoop down among the battery horse standing there apart. A half a dozen horses start, they stumble, their legs stiffen, their vitals and blood smear the ground. . . . We see the poor fellows hobbling back from the crest, or unable to do so, pale and weak and lying on the ground with the mangled stump of an arm or leg, dripping their life-blood away; or with a cheek torn open, or a shoulder mashed. . . .

Lee watched. War had patterns: like a shell exploding, a bright gleam of light radiating from a point and quickly followed by a small, white, puffy cloud. Big guns softened the resistance of the enemy so that other men, Pickett's men, could charge across those 1,400 yards with rifle and bayonet. It was nasty, brutal, and for some reason that only God understood necessary—here, at this instant, with Pickett's three little brigades poised. Those gray-clad lads, seeing Lee, were "thrilled and horrified." They yelled for him to go back. He turned, smiled, raised his hat. Then Pickett's boys charged at Gettysburg—among them Private John Dooley:

I tell you, there is no romance in making one of these charges. You might think so from reading "Charlie O'Malley," that prodigy of valour, or in reading of any other gallant knight who would as little think of riding over *gunners*

and such like as they would of eating a dozen oysters. But
when you rise to your feet as we did today, I tell you the
enthusiasm of ardent breasts in many cases *ain't there*, and
instead of burning to avenge the insults of our country, families and altars and firesides, the thought is most frequently,
*Oh, if I could just come out of this charge safely how thank-
ful would I be!*

We rise to our feet, but not all. There is a line of men
still on the ground with their faces turned, men affected in
four different ways. There are the gallant dead who will
never charge again; the helpless wounded, many of whom
desire to share the fortunes of the charge; the men who have
charged on many a battlefield but who are now helpless
from the heat of the sun; and the men in whom there is not
sufficient courage to enable them to rise. . . .

Up, brave men! . . . Onward—steady—dress to the
right—give way to the left—steady, not too fast—don't
press upon the center—how gentle the slope! steady—keep
well in line—there is the line of guns we must take—right
in front—but how far they appear! Nearly one third of a
mile, off on Cemetery Ridge, and the line stretches round
in almost a semicircle. Upon the center of this we must
march. Behind the guns are strong lines of infantry. You
may see them plainly and now they see us perhaps more
plainly.

. . . Directly in front of us, breathing flame in our very
faces, the long range of guns which must be taken thunder
on our quivering melting ranks. . . . The line becomes
unsteady because at every step a gap must be closed and thus
from left to right much ground is often lost. . . . Capt.
Hallinan has fallen and I take his place. So many men have
fallen now that I find myself within a few feet of my old
Captain. His men are pressing mine out of place. I ask him
to give way a little to the left, and scarcely has he done so
than he leaps into the air, falling prostrate. . . . Our men
are falling faster now, for the deadly musket is at work. Volley after volley of crushing musket balls sweeps through the
line and mows us down like wheat before the scythe.

On! men, on! Thirty yards more . . . but who can stand such a storm of hissing lead and iron? . . . Just here—from right to left the remnants of our braves pour in their long reserved fire; until now no shot had been fired, no shout of triumph had been raised; but as the cloud of smoke rises over the heads of the advancing divisions the well-known Southern battle cry which marks the victory gained or nearly gained bursts wildly over the blood stained field and *all that line of guns is ours.*

Shot through both thighs, I fall about thirty yards from the guns. By my side lies Lt. Kehoe, shot through the knee. Here we lie, he in excessive pain, I fearing to bleed to death, the dead and dying all around, while the division sweeps over the Yankee guns. Oh, how I long to know the re-sult. . . . There—listen—we hear a new shout, and cheer after cheer rends the air. Are those fresh troops advancing to our support? No! no! That huzza never broke from southern throats. Oh God!

Lee saw them coming back, knew what they had been through. For almost an hour he tried to speak to every soldier who passed. "Don't be discouraged," he cried. "It was my fault this time." Or: "Form your ranks when you get under cover." Or: "All good men must hold together now." The litter-bearers came by, carrying the wounded General Kemper, in whose brigade young Dooley served. "I hope you are not badly hurt," Lee said. Kemper replied: "I'm afraid they have got me this time." Lee pressed the general's hand: "I trust not! I trust not!" Lee seemed more father than commander. When an ordinance officer raised a stick to a balking horse, Lee spoke out: "Oh, don't do that! I once had a foolish horse and I found gentle measures so much the best."

Freemantle told Longstreet: "I wouldn't have missed this for anything."

Old Pete laughed. "The devil you wouldn't! I would

like to have missed it very much. We've attacked and been repulsed."

Freemantle admired Longstreet, thinking that "no person could have been more calm or self-possessed. . . . I could now fully appreciate the term bulldog, which I had heard applied to him by the soldiers." When a bri-gade commander complained that he was unable to bring up his troops, Longstreet answered with sarcasm: "Very well, never mind then, General. Just let them remain where they are. The enemy's going to advance and will spare you the trouble."

But where Longstreet retained his bite after the bloody charge that had gained so little except to hold for a few minutes some Federal guns, Lee reacted only with gentle kindliness. Jeb Stuart, who finally had reached Gettysburg the night before, had lost none of his bra-vado, but in his official report Lee wrote: "The move-ments of the army preceding the battle . . . had been much embarrassed by the absence of the cavalry." Yet even Jeb was somewhat more subdued by the evening of the 3rd; the Federal cavalry had licked him roundly in what the Yankee Pleasonton called "the finest cavalry fight of the war." George Edward Pickett, whose boys had died as perhaps only boys had died on the slopes of Marye's Heights, ended a letter to his wife: "Your Sol-dier lives and mourns and, but for you, my darling, he would rather, a million times rather, be back there with his dead, to sleep for all time in an unknown grave."

Yet Lee kept the initiative. On July 4, one of the blackest days for the Confederacy—that morning Vicks-burg surrendered to Grant—the gray columns of the Army of Northern Virginia began the homeward march along the Fairfield road. On the 6th Lee reached Wil-liamsport, and few knew how grieved he was by news that on the 29th of June a Federal raiding party had

swept down on Hickory Hill, capturing Rooney. Flood
tides in the Potomac found Lee entrenching desperately,
expecting pursuit and attack by Meade, but he worried
needlessly: Meade felt his army too exhausted to finish
the job (and Lincoln knew he still had not found his
general).

Back in Virginia, Lee rested and tried to see Gettysburg in perspective. He knew it was human to blame
others for disappointments and failures, a trait he could
only describe as "unbecoming in a generous person." He
had heard and read the criticisms of himself; quite
frankly, he wrote to Davis:

. . . No one is more aware than myself of my inability
for the duties of my position. I cannot even accomplish what
I myself desire. How can I fulfill the expectations of others?
In addition I sensibly feel the growing failure of my bodily
strength. I have not yet recovered from the attack I experienced the past spring. I am becoming more and more incapable of exertion, and am thus prevented from making the
personal examinations and giving the personal supervision
to the operations in the field which I feel to be necessary. I
am so dull making use of the eyes of others I am frequently
misled. Everything, therefore, points to the advantages to be
derived from a new commander, and I the more anxiously
urge the matter upon Your Excellency from my belief that
a younger and abler man than myself can readily be obtained. I know that he will have as gallant and brave an
army as ever existed to second his efforts, and it would be
the happiest day of my life to see at its head a worthy
leader—one that would accomplish more than I could per-
form and all that I have wished. . . .

Within three days the President replied. "There has
been nothing which I have found to require a greater
effort of patience," Davis confided to Lee, "than to bear
the criticisms of the ignorant, who pronounce everything

a failure which does not equal their expectations or de-
sires, and can see no good result which is not in line of
their own imaginings." Especially did he wish "the public journals were not generally partisan nor venal." It
would have been no effort for Lee, had he been willing
to stoop to it, to pamper his critics into exalting "you
for what you had not done rather than detract from the
achievements which will make you and your army the
subject of history and object of the world's admiration
for generations to come." To ask him to find a more capable leader for the Army of Northern Virginia than the
one it now had, Davis declared, was "to demand an im-
possibility."

CHAPTER ELEVEN

THEN CAME GRANT

AFTER Gettysburg, Lee camped along the Rapidan near Orange Court House, and Meade brought the Army of the Potomac to the vicinity of Culpeper. In succeeding months both armies were more like tired, cumbersome wrestlers than the vital, aggressive in-fighters of the spring and early summer. Cautiously they circled each other— grappling without too much spirit when forced into a clinch, then breaking away to stalk, to watch, to spar off any really decisive contact. Both armies detached units: Lee sending Longstreet's corps into Tennessee to help Bragg at Chickamauga, and Meade hurrying two divisions to New York City to assist in quelling the draft riots. November brought a vicious fight in the Wilderness at Mine Run, but neither side gained anything. At the year's end Lee and Meade had lumbered back to the Rapidan to hibernate through the winter not far from positions occupied before Second Manassas. Skill of maneuver both generals displayed, occasional cavalry and infantry raid annoyed the resting giants, but the dreary result could not be denied: Lee and Meade were stalemated.

The gentleness in Lee grew during the winter on the Rapidan; he became "a gray and simple soldier," riding among his troops "and smiling kindly as his eyes fell upon the tattered uniforms and familiar faces." To John Esten Cooke it seemed that "there was in this human being's character naught that was insincere, assumed or pretentious. . . . Other men reveal their weaknesses on nearer acquaintance—Lee only revealed his greatness, and he was more and more loved and admired." Edmund

Lee Childe testified: "The whole army felt that this man—so undemonstrative, so simply clad, sleeping like the commonest soldier in his tent, having in the midst of the wood a single blanket—was its guide, its protector, incessantly attentive to its welfare, jealous of its dearly purchased fame, and always ready, as its commander and friend, to defend it." Lee handled all complaints by telling an aide, " 'Suage him, Colonel, 'suage him"; and Colonel Venable enjoyed telling Richmond matrons how one of the merriest charges had concerned Jeb Stuart: "Some women wrote to complain of Stuart, whose horse the girls bedecked with garlands, and said he was in the habit of kissing girls. They thought General Stuart should be forbidden to kiss one unless he could kiss all." How Lee 'suaged this complaint, Venable did not say.

A letter from a private contended that short rations left him too fatigued to do his work, and in reply in late January Lee issued a general order, assuring the army that "no effort has been spared for its wants." He exhorted his men: "Soldiers! You tread with no unequal step the road by which your fathers marched through suffering, privations and blood, to independence. Continue to imitate in the future, as you have in the past, their valor in arms, their patient endurance of hardships, their high resolve to be free, which no trial could shake, no bribe seduce, no danger appall." If these words filled no bellies, they silenced the murmuring tongues.

More than ever religion swept the Army of Northern Virginia that winter, and Childe described "the affecting spectacle of old gray-bearded soldiers, devoutly kneeling in a circle"—conduct, he thought, natural "with men of the old English or Scotch race." A camp newspaper, the *Rapid Ann*, flourished briefly. One Alabamian wrote his wife of weather "as cold as the world's charity," and counted thirty-one men in Battle's brigade without "a sign of a shoe on their feet"; across the river one day Yankees, watching the baptism of a Southern soldier, joined in the hymn-singing.

Lee continued to worry over Rooney, now knowing the full story of what had happened at Hickory Hill—the Federals carrying Rooney out of the house on a mattress and whisking him away in a carriage to Fortress Monroe to hold as a hostage for the safety of captive Federal officers. Yet when a Federal officer in Libby Prison begged Lee to arrange an exchange of Rooney for himself, Lee shook his head—he would ask no favor for his son that he could not secure for any soldier in the army—and Colonel Long felt he never had seen such a demonstration of "the lofty spirit of a Roman Brutus." But winter brought a sad change when Rooney's wife, the vivacious former Charlotte Wickham, fell ill. Custis offered to take his brother's place in prison so that Rooney could see Charlotte before she died; the request was refused. Lee lived in misery; he was devoted to his daughter-in-law.

There were frequent visits to Richmond. The Confederate capital was filled with feelings of guilt for its gaiety, but the parties went on. The laugh of the season was a story about angels who flew down to lead Stonewall Jackson into heaven and found that by a rapid flank movement Jackson already had cut his way in; and the pointed quip scored high prices and deflated Confederate currency: "You take your money to market in the market basket, and bring home what you buy in your pocketbook." Mrs. Chesnut, also spending the winter in Richmond, declared that the charges of social frivolity did not apply to Mary Lee: "Her room was like an industrial school, with everybody so busy. Her daughters were all there, plying their needles, and also several other ladies. . . . What a rebuke to the taffy parties!"

Not the least question existed in Mrs. Chesnut's mind
as to the position Lee occupied on these visits to Richmond—he was "the very first man in the world." The
portrait drawn of the Lee family in Richmond paralleled
the pictures of the general with his army. Certainly there
was no affectation in Lee, laughing at Custis sleeping on
the floor so that his poor old father could have a bed.
Mary remained cheerful in her wheelchair but Con-
stance Cary whispered to Mrs. Chesnut: "If it pleased
God to take poor Cousin Mary Lee—she suffers so—
wouldn't these Richmond women campaign for Cousin
Robert?" Meanwhile, thought Mrs. Chesnut, "Cousin
Robert" held all admiring females at arm's length.

Rooney was released from prison and back in Richmond by mid-March. Tears filled Lee's eyes at any mention of Charlotte. Rooney annoyed Richmond propa-
gandists by declaring that Ben "Beast" Butler had used
him rather decently in prison and had even sent him his
horse. "The Lees are men enough to speak the truth of
friend and foe, not fearing consequences," thought Mrs.
Chesnut. But Richmond was so endeared to gossip that
when one Sunday fourteen generals were found in
church, Lee among them, many wondered if "less piety
and more drilling of commands [might not] suit the times
better." Bad blood boiled between Lee and old Wade
Hampton, who grumbled that Stuart had taken one of
his brigades and given it to Fitzhugh Lee. "I would not
care if you went back to South Carolina with your whole
division," a mortified Hampton quoted Lee as saying;
least disturbed was Fitzhugh, delighted with a toy
Negro boy which, when wound up, danced minstrel
fashion.

The event that winter which would change the lives
of everyone in Richmond occurred in Washington. In
early March a squat man and a gangling boy registered

at Willard's Hotel: "U. S. Grant and Son, Galena, Ill." Then on the evening of the 8th the man went to the White House to pay his respects to the President, unaware that a reception was in progress or that he would all but turn that affair into a shambles. Lincoln was never much to look at even in evening dress—turned-down collar invariably a size too large, necktie askew, face sad, ungainly figure towering over the other heads around him—but Lincoln's six feet four inches allowed him that evening to recognize his self-conscious visitor and to call out: "Why, here is General Grant!"

So face to face, shaking hands, the two "uncommon common men" met for the first time, both men who had risen to great power from humble beginnings. Grant had just been named lieutenant general and placed in charge of all Union armies, a command of more than a half-million men. Cabinet officers, foreign emissaries, senators, congressmen climbed onto sofas and chairs, chanting: "Grant! Grant! Grant!" as they tried to catch a glimpse of the general. An hour passed before Lincoln and the Secretary of War could shepherd Grant into a drawing-room.

In Lee's letters there are few references to Lincoln: surely he could not understand a man about whom he rarely thought, and he could not beat the North without understanding Lincoln. Lee had a keen knowledge of the men who had opposed him in the field: McClellan, who would write letters saying he believed he could be made dictator, but who possessed no heart for risking his kingdom; Pope, who was a bluff, and McDowell, who was simply a competent mediocrity; Burnside, who was sick, stubborn, and foolish; Hooker, with outthrust chest and soft belly; Meade, competent, manly, and as unimaginative as any turtle in a shell.

Lincoln knew that each had misused and abused the

greatest fighting force ever created on the American continent; had there been one Lee among them, the war
should have been over. Nor could the superior resources
of the North alone explain why the Army of Northern
Virginia and the Army of the Potomac now were stalled
in virtual stalemate; Lee thought this was the reason, but
Lee was wrong. There also had been a superb wholeness
in Lincoln—a broad, sweeping vision that had grasped
the military, political, psychological, and philosophical
necessities of the great American conflict—and the backbone to resist discouragement in battle and intimidation
in Congress, on the border, in Europe. After all these
years, Lincoln fought without malice or bitterness for
one purpose, one country, of which Lee and his army remained essentially a part.

In Grant, too, there was a wholeness, a dogged resolution to repress a rebellion and nothing more—certainly
none of the political ambition that forever nibbled at Mc-
Clellan, and none of the vanity of a Frémont that so
confused civil and military authority. From complete obscurity, Grant simply had kept coming on, always a bit
better than anyone had suspected, making his own opportunities when no one seemed to want to let him fight—
smashing his way out of a trap at Belmont, swiping Pa-
ducah from under the eyes of Bishop Polk, winning a
hero's adulation with his "unconditional surrender" at
Donelson, slipping when caught napping at Shiloh, then
daring, brilliant, a man of unmistakable success in winning Vicksburg, Missionary Ridge.

With his slouching, unmilitary gait, his squint eyes,
his shaggy beard and easygoing manner, Grant looked
neither a general nor a poet, yet in temperament he happened to be both. He was a thinker, a planner, a general
at his best tipped back on a camp stool, eyes half-closed;
he could write out an order in crisp, clear sentences; and

since boyhood he had been haunted by an obsession against ever taking a backward step. He was deeply, passionately sensitive, and given to fits of melancholy when too long separated from an adored wife: then he might drink too much for his own good, and ten times too much for the good of any average man. In the morning he would be clearheaded: it was unbelievable. Men and officers learned to trust, to love him; his own philosophy of war could be reduced to four words: "When in doubt, fight." Soldiers said of him: "Ulysses don't scare worth a damn"; and William T. Sherman, who knew and loved him as much as anyone in the army, predicted that when Grant reached Virginia, "the fur would fly."

Lincoln wanted nothing more. After that first reception, the President invited Grant to dinner and was firmly refused. "I have become very tired of this show business," the general said. Lincoln wondered about Phil Sheridan, whom Grant had brought from the West to handle his cavalry; he seemed "rather a little fellow." Quietly, Grant answered: "You will find him big enough for the purpose before we get through with him." Lincoln looked down, not taking the measure of this man as he had done with all the others, but smiling. He had found his man and intended to leave him alone. On March 26 Grant arrived at Culpeper.

Lee put happy recollections of Richmond behind him. Reports from spies in April sifted through his hands. A main assault was coming across the Rapidan, a diversion into the Valley, and an attack somewhere on the flank or rear—so Lee fitted the pieces together and read Grant's mind. Where would the troops gathering on the Chesapeake be thrown? Against Drewry's Bluff on the James, Lee guessed. This flanking movement troubled him most; if it could be met, he said: "I have no uneasiness as to the result of the campaign in Virginia." As for the main assault, Lee told Davis, if Beauregard's army could be brought east to defend Richmond, then the Army of Northern Virginia should "move against the enemy on the Rappahannock" and "should God give us a crowning victory there, all their plans would be dissipated, and their troops now collecting on the waters of the Chesapeake would be recalled to the defense of Washington."

It was a brave dream, but Lee must confess weaknesses. To make such a move he must have forage and provisions—where would he get them? He must have aggressive supporting action in the west and some peace of mind over a continuing Federal threat to Charleston—what miracle would produce these? Longstreet, now back from Tennessee, had Pickett's division in the vicinity of Petersburg; with the greatest effort, Lee might scrape together a shade better than 60,000 effectives to match Grant's 125,000 or more. And an imponderable remained—just how good was Grant? In late April Lee wrote Custis, not concealing his uneasiness: "If I could get back Pickett, Hoke and R. Johnston I would feel strong enough to operate." Lee took his field glasses and rode up Clark's Mountain to see what the Federals were doing under Grant's prodding. By May 2 he thought he knew what the Union command intended—a movement across the fords at Ely's and Germanna.

Lee took heart—those fords led into the Wilderness, where Hooker, despite his vastly superior numbers, had floundered miserably. Why wouldn't Grant do as badly? In a cheerful spirit Lee told Colonel Taylor that the Army of Northern Virginia never had been in better trim: "There is no overweening confidence, but a calm, firm and positive determination to be victorious, with God's help." Again he wrote Custis: "If victorious, we have everything to hope for in the future. If defeated,

nothing will be left for us to live for. . . . My whole
trust is in God, and I am ready for whatever He may
ordain."

Moving across the Rapidan at Ely's and Germanna,
Grant could not understand why the passage of the Federal troops was uncontested. This was a great success, he
told Washington, crossing the river "in the face of an
active, large, well-appointed and ably-commanded
army." Lee smiled and permitted his opponent to plunge
into the dense thickets of the sunless forest, into this
friendless realm of the owl, the whippoorwill, and the
moccasin. As Grant established his army in the upper
part of the Wilderness of Spotsylvania, Lee concentrated
at Mine Run, about four miles northwest of Grant. Longstreet was still twenty miles away that evening of May 4
when Lee gazed across the somber region. Where was
the ghost of Jackson, if not here?

At breakfast next morning Lee was cheerful, teasing
his staff, content in backing Grant into the Wilderness
and, said Long, expressing surprise "that his new adversary had placed himself in the same predicament as
Fighting Joe." He hoped "the result would be even more
disastrous to Grant." Late that afternoon Federal right
and Confederate left clashed in a bitter, inconclusive
fight that nightfall ended, and a surprised Grant learned a
lesson—the fight next day would see his whole army in
line of battle. The thread gloves that Mrs. Grant had
forced him to wear in recognition of his new rank had
now, thank God, worn out; it was newness enough
learning how to handle "a battle fought with the ear, and
not with the eye."

The restlessness of Grant, the restlessness of Lee found
both armies moving at dawn on the 6th. Twenty yards
off, one antagonist could not see the other, and, said a
spirited contemporary account:

. . . Death came unseen; regiments stumbled on each
other and sent swift destruction into each other's ranks,
guided by the crackling of the bushes. It was not war—military maneuvering; science had as little to do with it as sight.
Two wild animals were hunting each other; when they
heard each other's steps they sprung and grappled. The conqueror advanced, or went elsewhere. The dead were lost
from all eyes in the thicket. . . . Officers advanc[ed] to
the charge in the jungle, *compass in hand.* . . . Here in
blind wrestle as at midnight did two hundred thousand men
in blue and gray clutch each other—bloodiest and weirdest
of encounters. War had had nothing like it. . . .

Lee suffered through the day, waiting for Longstreet.
Even in this ungodly hole Lee had a sound plan, intending to demonstrate heavily against the Federal right so
that Old Pete, coming up, could drive the full force of
his center and right against the Federal left, seize the
Brock Road to southward, and throw Grant's left wing
back into the thickets around Chancellorsville. The
plan's weakness developed in the stubborn resistance on
the Federal left, where Hill, furiously engaged on front
and flank, fell back steadily for a considerable distance.
But Longstreet arrived, supported Hill, flung the Yankees back to their original position on the Brock Road.

Lee was elated as Longstreet's boys crashed into the
fight. "Whose troops are they?" he called. Law's Alabama brigade, he was told. "God bless the Alabamians!"
Lee cried, and heard the men go forward with a whoop.
Texans, finding the general too close to the front, yelled:
"Go back, General Lee! Go back!" A sergeant seized his
bridle rein. There was in Lee now that "subdued excitement" that Longstreet sometimes distrusted, that response
when "the hunt was up."

Yet who could blame him? It looked as though Longstreet would gain the Brock Road, that the plan would

work. He had "another Bull Run on them," Longstreet shouted, but Old Pete had not reckoned on one calamity. Turning to go back, for he was riding in front of his own advancing lines, the general was mistaken by his own men for a Federal cavalry rider. A musket-ball disabled Longstreet, threw his advance into disorder, and Lee, hastening forward to take personal command, couldn't regain the impetus. Fire in a thicket encircled the antagonists in roaring flame, but the bloody horror went on— went on till darkness without decision. Grant was shocked by the brutal fight, and, said a witness, watching Grant go into his tent that night and throw himself face downward on his cot: "I never saw a man so agitated in my life." Lee, too, was jarred, hurt, unhappy. The two giants had taken first measure of one another—in the magnificent phrase of John Esten Cooke, Grant with his hammer and Lee with his rapier—and now they knew: this was the climax of all the years of blood and toil, this was for keeps, the victory or, as Lee had written Custis four days before, the defeat in which "nothing will be left for us to live for."

Grant made the next logical move, trying to get behind and beyond Lee's right flank on the way to Richmond—his famous "sidling" by the left flank—moving toward Hanover by way of Spotsylvania Court House. Here for twelve days Lee and Grant locked in the first trench warfare, Grant giving up three casualties for one of Lee's (yet being able to afford to, the fact that staggered Lee), and producing on the salient north of the pretty white-columned courthouse the grimmest hand-to-hand fighting of the war—the now legendary Bloody Angle. What was happening to Grant, a member of Congress asked Lincoln, and the President replied: "Well, I can't tell much about it. You see, Grant has gone into the Wilderness, crawled in, drawn up the ladder, and pulled in the hole after him, and I guess we'll have to wait till he comes out before we know just what he's up to." Lee rallied his troops, took reckless chance after reckless chance to cheer them, to keep up their spunk, and the spirit of his men was expressed by the gray-clad who, ending an argument on atheism, said: "Well, boys, the rest of us may have developed from monkeys; but I tell you none less than a God could have made such a man as Marse Robert!"

Yet Lee was deeply troubled. Sheridan was riding toward Richmond, drawing Stuart's cavalry off Grant's flanks, smashing the railroad at Beaver Dam Station, meeting Jeb six miles north of Richmond at Yellow Tavern on the 8th. A pistol-shot ripped Stuart's abdomen; comrades carried him to Richmond to die. The army under Butler that had been sent to the James was being outmarched by Beauregard, a cheerful note—in disgust, Grant saw Butler "in a bottle tightly corked," and this was a predicament Grant did not fancy for himself. On May 20 Grant again "sidled"—left across the North Anna, left, irresistibly left, seeing in his mind's eye the James, Richmond.

Pickett's division, Hoke's old brigade, Breckinridge's forces came up, giving Lee another 8,500 men. With Grant's army hung half one side and half the other of the North Anna, could Lee strike a blow that would truly hurt his adversary? Lee lay in his tent, stricken with a violent intestinal illness, losing his temper so that Venable, coming out red-faced, blurted: "I have just told the old man that he is not fit to command this army, and that he had better send for Beauregard." Lee clenched his fist against the pain; he was not beaten, he would not be beaten; Grant was slipping away now through luck, because there was no one to direct an attack—not old Ewell, or Hill who had been bludgeoned at Spotsylvania, or Dick Anderson, who scarcely had learned how to pull the ropes of Longstreet's command. Alone in the tent, Lee groaned. He wasn't afraid of Grant or awed by Grant. When Dr. Gwathmey came in, Lee muttered: "If I can get one more pull at him, I will defeat him."

Grant, putting back the ladder and the hole and emerging from the Wilderness, refused to meet Lee between the North and South Anna but moved on to the south side of the Pamunkey. "Lee's army is really whipped," Grant told Washington, making as bad a guess as he ever would.

The armies had come back to Cold Harbor—Old Cold Harbor, some of Lee's veterans called it, rolling back the memory of two years to the Battle of the Seven Days against McClellan. Then Lee had been tricked by faulty maps; now he knew how to entrench on every ridge, how to get the advantage from every stream, every inch of swamp. Here, if Grant wanted to be stubborn and drive a frontal attack in the hope of gaining the north side of the James and capturing Richmond perhaps without siege, Lee believed that he could trim him. For Grant the choice was hard; not to fight meant moving south to the James and operating in the vicinity of Petersburg. Waiting, Yankee Colonel Theodore Lyman thought of Lee: "He is a brave and skillful soldier and will fight while he has a division or a day's rations left. These Rebels are not half-starved—a more sinewy, tawny, formidable-looking set of men could not be." Grant's decision was to continue his "smash-'em-up" policy; as the order for attack reached the Federals, Horace Porter found the men "calmly writing their names and home addresses on slips of paper and pinning them on the back of their coats, so that their dead bodies might be recognized and their fates made known to their families at home."

A wise precaution this proved for many—Cold Harbor would rank among the bloodiest slaughters of the war as 10,000 of Grant's best soldiers were lost. The precision with which Lee set his stage for that slaughter is detailed in the official records, but these are dead lines, devoid of the flaming emotion of history in volcanic eruption upon the five acres of this battleground. Not so the simple sentences of Captain James M. Nichols of the 48th New York Volunteers: "It was a dreadful place to hold, with the Rebels pouring in upon us a deadly flanking fire. . . . Back through the woods we went, broken and dispirited." Not so the account of Robert Stiles, Confederate artillery officer:

We were in line of battle at Cold Harbor from the first to the twelfth of June—say twelve days. The battle proper did not last perhaps that many minutes. In some respects at least it was one of the notable battles of history—certainly in its brevity measured in time and its length measured in slaughter, as also in the disproportion of the losses. For my own part, I would scarcely say whether it lasted eight or sixty minutes, or eight or sixty hours, all my powers being concentrated on keeping the guns supplied with ammunition.

Here, then, is the secret of the otherwise inexplicable butchery. A little after daylight on June 3, 1864, along the line of our salient, our infantry and our artillery fired at very short range into a mass of men twenty-eight deep, who could neither advance nor retreat, and the most of whom could not even discharge their muskets at us.

Federal writers . . . speak about our works as bastions no troops could have been expected to take . . . [but] I helped with my own hands to make them, I fought behind them. They were a single line of earth four feet high and three to five feet thick. . . . There was no physical difficulty in walking right over that ditch. . . .

I wonder if it could have been the *men* behind the works!

Lee knew. This army could fight. It could take any frontal attack Grant wanted to mount—take it on the right, where Hoke commanded; and in the center where Finegan's Florida brigade and the Maryland Line bolstered Breckinridge's wavering ranks . . . these were cool veterans with steady nerves who had been through a lot of war with Lee. Grimly, Grant said afterward: "I regret this assault more than any one I have ever ordered." Grant's "smash-'em-up" policy hadn't budged or buckled Lee; now Federal officers began asking Grant—Rawlins, Dana, men on his staff—could *they* continue to take it or ultimately would they (as General James H. Wilson remembered) "so decimate and discourage the rank and file that they could not be induced to face the enemy at all?"

Grant admitted his respect for Lee—by deed rather than by word. On June 15 the race for Petersburg began.

CHAPTER TWELVE

THE ROAD TO APPOMATTOX

ALL through the summer, the fall, the bleak, chill winter Petersburg lay under siege. In 1860, census figures set the population of this city on the south bank of the Appomattox River at 18,266. The tracks of five railroad lines radiated from Petersburg—the Richmond and Petersburg ran north, the Weldon south to North Carolina, the Norfolk and Petersburg southwest, the Petersburg and City Point to the confluence of the James and the Appomattox eight miles distant, and the Richmond and Danville to the capital twenty-three miles north. McClellan had been alert to the significance of Petersburg as the back door to Richmond and had pleaded for the opportunity to carry his campaign from the Peninsula to this railhead when orders had turned him back to Washington and the tragedy of Second Manassas. Now Grant was here, locked in a death struggle with Lee along a ten-mile front, determined that if he couldn't smash-'em-up he would sit-'em-out.

Fierce fighting from mid-June 1864 into late February 1865 kept the Petersburg front anything but static— the savage action at the Crater, the two battles before Grant gained the Weldon Railroad, the fighting at Reams Station, Peeble's Farm, Cedar Creek, Burgess Mill, the Boydton Plank Road. Lee had been a great general before; now he rose to magnificence, already an emergent legend, the tongues of his critics stilled, Congress eager to make him the military dictator of the Confederacy, the adoration of soldiers shared by the vast majority of civilians. If Jackson had seemed a saint, Lee became little less than a god—he was now the "Noble Lee," the man who could still smile, who was selfless in his compassion for others, the old gray warrior in the armor of a shining heart.

Everyone knew the hardships he bore, the despair he suffered, the tragedy he foresaw in the misery of his soul; yet he was the general who would get down from Traveller on a cold November day and say to a flushed-faced lieutenant: "My boy, let me show you how to make a fire." Stooping, he pulled the wood open at the top, had the coals and kindling from underneath placed in the opening. "This is the way," he said good-humoredly, "the old servants showed me how to make a fire when I was a boy." With his calmness, his composure, there grew this depth of good nature; Mrs. Davis, serving him *café au lait* in a fine Sèvres cup, would hear: "My cups in camp are thicker, but this is thinner than the coffee."

Soldiers in the trenches around Petersburg knew Lee best, and believed the two maxims that summed up his philosophy: "Do your duty" and "Human virtue should be equal to human calamity." Any tattered private could approach him without hesitancy or embarrassment; he was one of them, had grown old in the bitter struggle with them, and inspired a confidence that amounted to superstition. The illness following Spotsylvania had left him—"he seemed made of iron," said John Esten Cooke, "and would remain in his saddle all day and then at his desk half the night without apparently feeling any fatigue." The poet Sidney Lanier saw Lee gently sleeping at outdoor church services: "Not a muscle of him stirred, not a nerve of his grand countenance twitched, there was no drooping of the head nor bowing of the figure. . . . As he slumbered so, sitting erect with his arms folded upon his chest in an attitude of majestic repose such as I never saw assumed by mortal man before . . . it seemed to me as if the present earth floated off through the sunlight and the antique earth returned out of the past and some majestic god sat on a hill sculptured in stone presiding over a terrible yet sublime contest of human passions." So did the legend of Lee take root—in the heart of a soldier trying to build a fire, over a Sèvres cup, through the eyes of a novelist, on the lips of a poet.

Visitors to Petersburg today see first the Crater, where Yankee and Rebel fought on a hot July 30, and it is easily the most dramatic incident of the long siege, the point at which emerged anew the everlasting fight in Lee as long as there was hope. The idea of blowing up a section of Confederate entrenchments by tunneling and mining the place belonged to Henry Pleasants of the 48th Pennsylvania, an old civil engineer. For almost a month tunnels were dug—a main shaft over five hundred feet, above an air tube—Pleasants dogged in his will, sending to a sawmill outside the lines when timber was refused him, using cracker boxes to carry away the dirt when he could secure no wheelbarrows. On July 27 eight thousand pounds of powder were placed under the Confederate entranchments. A fuse sputtered out on the first attempt three days later to explode the charge, and two volunteers, as indefatigable as Pleasants, crawled into the shaft to repair it. Then the whole length of fuse ignited and the earth shot upward, mixed with flame, with lightning flashes, with torn timbers and bits of human bodies.

Up billowed the hot white smoke and gray dust, a cloud that hung over a crater 200 feet long, 50 feet wide, perhaps 30 feet deep, where moments before had stood a Confederate redan. Rebel troops fled, leaving a gap, all the Yankees should need to gain the hill. But the Federals marched into the crater and became bogged in pits and cut-up trenches—three brigades utterly confused, white troops and Negroes. The Rebels came back, holding their fire till the Yankees came out of their self-made hole, taking a tip from Revolutionary days and waiting till they could see the whites of their eyes, ending in a fierce hand-to-hand struggle that drove the blue-clads back over the crest and into a plunging crossfire. After the wounded were carried out, 55 Negro dead and 178 whites were buried by the Rebels. Such was the Battle of the Crater; it changed nothing.

The August sun was hot, September and October pleasant, November filled with the portents of approaching winter. The siege continued with Federal and Confederate lines sometimes only yards apart and separated by two miles at their widest point. Early marched into the Valley—the old game of frightening Washington, which always had worked—and came back, beaten, the Valley lost forever. Jumping off from Dalton, Sherman ran the flanks of Johnston's army to Atlanta, smashed his way into the city, then struck out on his march to the sea—or, as Grant said, disappeared like a ground mole under a lawn: "You can here and there trace his track, but you are not quite certain where he will come out till you see his head."

War Clerk Jones, sensing the end, lived in misery: in July he cooked the part of the chicken a cat hadn't eaten; in August he snapped at the Secretaries of State and the Navy and the Postmaster General, who "are getting as fat as bears, while some of the subordinates I know of are becoming mere shadows from scarcity of food"; in September he reported the Governor of Georgia "bitterly and offensively" criticizing the President's handling of military affairs and demanding the return of Georgian troops to defend their own state; in December he felt Davis was "incapacitated both mentally and physically by disease" and could hardly express his scorn for a Congress that "wastes its time in discussions on the

adoption of a *flag* for future generations." Winter found
Confederate Treasury notes worth less than two cents on
the dollar, desertions increasing, and Congress debating a
bill to arm slaves.

Lee was deeply interested in this legislation; he wrote
Congressman Barksdale: "Under good officers and good
instructions, I do not see why they should not become
soldiers." He urged "the condition of emancipation" for
all who enrolled; but the bill, finally passed in March
1865, avoided any promise of freedom—it became a
question whether there was a realist left in official Richmond. Surely Senator W. S. Oldham of Texas was not
one, when in a remarkably bland speech he told his col-
leagues late in January: "It has recently been my duty,
as Senators know, to look into the military resources of
our country, and I unhesitatingly declare that they are
ample to enable us to maintain ourselves indefinitely
against any force the enemy can bring against us." Nor
was Jefferson Davis any vast realist when that same month
he agreed to appoint a commission "with a view to secure peace to the two countries." Lincoln reminded him
that the objective in Washington was "securing peace to
the people of our *one common* country." Why should
Lincoln give up the point of the war at this late date?

The pitiful, painful death throes of the Confederacy
continued. Before Petersburg, Confederates slipped into
town to dance with the girls, scampered back to the
trenches when the firing heightened, then, declared William M. Owen, returned in the next lull to ask: "You
have kept the dance for me, Miss ——? Only a small
affair: one man killed, that's all." Perhaps. This wasn't
the Petersburg Lee knew. Colonel Marshall of his staff
could supply an interlude of amusement on the horse
that moved around in a sort of waltz the hotter the firing
became; poor Marshall had been sent a circus horse.

Oftener Lee's meditations more closely paralleled those of Lieutenant R. M. Collins: "Why is it that 200,000 men of one blood and one tongue, believing as one man in the fatherhood of God and the universal brotherhood of man, should in the nineteenth century of the Christian era be thus armed with all the appliances of modern warfare and seeking one another's lives? We could settle our differences by compromising and all be at home in ten days."

From the beginning of the siege Lee had warned Davis: "Put no reliance in what I can do individually, for I believe that will be very little." Despite the remarkable oration of Senator Oldham shortages of food, coupled with the phenomenal mismanagement of the Confederate Commissariat, brought the army to the verge of famine. Lee invariably had to scamper around to find a small piece of meat to serve a visitor to headquarters; officers took ground corn and shucks from the horses and fed them to the men.

Occasionally Lee went to Richmond, where Custis was in command; he would talk to the ailing Davis on his couch, telling him the truth about the grim conditions at Petersburg. Usually he stayed with the troops, inquiring of an officer: "Colonel, have you seen Rooney Lee lately? I didn't know but you had, Colonel; he is a gay young fellow like yourself. I thought maybe you had seen him last evening at that ball you attended in the city." Lee had no heart for social life now; he had hungry men in trenches of whom to think—and not enough men. He proposed to Davis a sort of commando raid into Maryland, using artillery, dismounted cavalry, and infantry to invade Point Lookout, where Confederates were held in prison. "By throwing them suddenly on the beach with some concert of action among the prisoners," he wrote, "I think the guard might be overpowered, the prisoners liberated and organized, and marched immediately on the route to Washington." Again, he dreamed of joining with the remnant of Joe Johnston's force in North Carolina.

Spring came on. The Union General Ben Butler was filled with ingenious schemes for lifting the siege of Petersburg. He proposed getting a gun that would shoot seven miles and, taking direction by compass, burn the city of Richmond with shells of Greek fire. "If that didn't do," declared Colonel Theodore Lyman, "he had an auger to bore a tunnel five feet in diameter, and he was going to bore to Richmond and suddenly pop up in somebody's basement while the family were at breakfast!"

Grant took an eminently more military view. He didn't know why Lee clung to the hopeless defense of Petersburg and every morning was afraid "I would awake to hear that Lee had gone." Why didn't Lee run south by way of the railroad through Danville? "If he got the start, the war might be prolonged another year," Grant thought, genuinely worried. As soon as the roads were passable, and Sheridan's cavalry joined him, Grant intended to move.

Lee saw Davis. The evacuation of Petersburg was only a question of time, Lee said; in the hope of compelling Grant to move around the Confederates in order to protect his line of communication with City Point, Lee planned his attack on Fort Stedman. What Lee sought, Davis explained, was to "relieve our right and delay the impending disaster until the more convenient season for retreat."

Lee launched his attack before daylight on March 25, throwing forces under John B. Gordon across the two hundred yards that separated Confederate and Yankee lines and gaining the garrison at Stedman by surprise. A detachment was sent to seize the high ground and works behind the fort so that Grant's batteries could be turned into the gorges right and left upon his own lines. In the foggy dawn the guides misled the detachment. Grant came back with heavy forces and flaming guns. Lee was licked, thoroughly.

Grant's counterstroke followed. Leaving a part of his army to hold the lines at Petersburg, he moved to the southwest and speeded Sheridan's cavalry up the road leading northwest from Dinwiddie to Five Forks. Thus, while Sheridan menaced Lee's right, Grant jockeyed for position to get up the Southside Railroad, and ultimately the Danville line, without which neither Petersburg nor Richmond could be held.

Lee knew the moment was desperate; he hustled Pickett with five brigades to Five Forks, and, in character, Lee said: get there first, take the offensive. Pickett was across the road when Sheridan came riding up on the 30th; he handled the Federals roughly, and drove Sheridan back down the road toward Dinwiddie. Next day Pickett and Fitzhugh Lee fought to within a hundred yards of Dinwiddie, then were forced back. "Hold Five Forks at all hazards," Lee ordered Pickett again that night.

Meanwhile ebullient Tom Rosser, a young giant who quarreled when he couldn't have his pretty wife with him at the front, had stopped two days before, while bringing up his brigade, to catch a mess of shad in the Nottoway River. Now he invited Pickett and Fitzhugh Lee to join him in a shad bake; the two generals accepted, and Fitzhugh Lee ignored warnings of heavy picket action as he anticipated his fish. So Pickett and Fitzhugh Lee were eating their shad when Sheridan came back, hell-on-leather this time, catching the pair flat-footed. Pickett, who had told his wife that except for her he wished he could have died at Gettysburg, forgot to mention the shad in his letter, describing his activities on reaching Five Forks:

I immediately formed line of battle and set my men to throwing up temporary breastworks. The men, God bless them, though weary and hungry, sang as they felled and dug. Three times in three hours their labors were suspended because of attack from the front, but they as cheerily returned to their digging and to their "Annie Laurie" and "Dixie" as if they were banking roses for a festival.

Five Forks is situated in a flat, thickly wooded country and is simply a crossing at right angles of two country roads and a deflection of a third bisecting one of these angles. Our line of battle, short as four small brigades' front must be, could readily be turned on either flank by a larger attacking force [Rosser, catching shad in a borrowed seine, had not arrived]. Do you understand, my dear? If not, you will some day.

Well, I made the best arrangements of which the ground admitted. About two o'clock in the afternoon [while he and Fitzhugh were picking the shad off the bones], Sheridan made a heavy demonstration with his cavalry, threatening also the right flank. Meantime Warren's corps swept around the left flank and rear of the infantry line, and the attack became general.

I succeeded in getting a sergeant and enough men to man one piece, but after their firing eight rounds the axle broke. One regiment fought hand to hand after all their cartridges had been used. The small cavalry force, which had got into place, gave way, and the enemy poured in. . . . We were completely entrapped. . . .

My darling, overpowered, defeated, cut in pieces, starving, captured, as we were, those that were left of us formed front north and south and met with sullen desperation their double onset. With the members of my own staff and the general officers and their staff officers we compelled a rally enabling many of us to escape capture.

The birds were hushed in the woods when I started to write, now one calls to its mate, "Cheer up—cheer up." Let's listen and obey the birds, my darling.

Worried soldiers, distracted officers at Lee's headquarters next morning, were muttering: disaster, ruin, the end! It was a dreadful blow, losing Five Forks. Lee appeared—calm, in full uniform, wearing his dress sword. Did he expect to be compelled to surrender that morning? Federal infantry in heavy column seemed dangerously close; a Confederate horse battery rumbled down the hill to escape capture. Musketry fire forced the infantry back, the artillery. Lee mounted Traveller. An aide heard Lee say: "This is a bad business, Colonel." He rode a little way, musing to himself. Then: "Well, Colonel, it has happened as I told them it would at Richmond. The line has been stretched until it has broken."

So, on April 2, the weary retreat began . . . Petersburg abandoned, Richmond lost . . . and yet in Lee a strain of the fighting bulldog remained. "I have got my army safe out of the breastworks," he said. "In order to follow me the enemy must abandon his lines and can derive no further benefit from his railroads or James River." In a Hooker—in a Beauregard, to keep the score even—the remark might have smacked of braggadocio. But Lee throbbed with hope. He already had ordered supplies from Richmond to Amelia Court House for just this emergency. With his army fed and provisioned, he would break through somehow, reach Lynchburg, join Johnston in North Carolina.

Lee's shattered army followed him gamely, though there were incidents like that when General Gordon inquired of a gray-clad boy why he was running and received the shouted reply: "Golly, I'm running 'cause I can't fly!" Behind them they could easily visualize the scenes in tormented Richmond: Federals clattering

through the streets, houses in flames, brokenhearted
women prisoners in their own homes or at night stealing
like shadows along the streets. For gaunt soldiers, bellies
thin from living for days on quarter rations, wobbling
legs were strengthened by the promise of stores at Amelia
Court House.

And then the crushing, devastating blow—half-starved
men, delayed by high water in the Appomattox, tramped
on behind Lee to discover that Richmond had failed
them, there were no stores! "Anxious and haggard" all
at once was Lee's face. The hopelessness of their situation smote him. Now they must halt, with Grant's thousands moving on them, to forage for food. Around were
straggling woods, pine barrens, patches of open ground—
how overwhelmingly futile it seemed! How many for-
agers would return, when the enemy's cavalry might
pop up from every mudhole or the chance given to desert
became irresistible? On the 5th and 6th hundreds of men
dropped to the ground from sheer exhaustion. Muskets
were thrown aside—they were too heavy to carry. On
the 7th, the 8th, the misery continued . . . men, chewing parched corn, complained of gums made sore and
bloody; whole wagon trains burned by the roadside
where they had been abandoned; yet the trancelike plod-
ding forward continued until, said Private Carlton Mc-
Carthy, "night was day—day was night."

After the first shock at Amelia Court House, Lee regained his spirit and composure. He spoke anew of
reaching Lynchburg, of joining Johnston. When Federal
cavalry forays stampeded his troops, and officers seemed
helpless, he went himself into the ranks, rallying his
men, urging: "That is right, men. Just keep those people
back a little while." It was brave and it was vain. At Saylor's Creek Sheridan's cavalry struck Ewell's corps,
hacked it terribly in an uneven contest, captured Ewell,

destroyed four hundred wagons, seized sixteen artillery pieces. The debacle at Saylor's Creek ended on the 7th; Grant that evening wrote Lee to end the needless blood-letting. Lee faced the bitter bargain: what were Grant's terms? Next morning Grant replied: ". . . there is but one condition I would insist upon—namely, that the men and officers surrendered shall be disqualified from taking up arms against the Government of the United States until properly exchanged. I will meet you at any point agreeable to you. . . ."

That evening Lee met with his generals. Blankets spread on the ground, saddles propped against the roots of trees, a low-burning bivouac fire—these were their accommodations. Lee looked down at the anguished faces; they, said General Gordon, looked back at "the clouded face of their beloved leader." But Lee's voice was calm, discussing his correspondence with Grant, what surrender would mean to the South. Then the decision was reached: at daylight they would cut their way through Grant's lines!

The attack failed, for all the heart and ferocity that supported it, for all that the Union breastworks were carried and two pieces of field artillery captured, for all that the Federals were driven from a portion of the field . . . David no longer possessed the stone to slay Goliath. Choked, Lee said: "There is nothing left me but to go and see General Grant, and I had rather die a thousand deaths." On April 9 he put on full uniform, embroidered belt and dress sword, tall hat, buff gauntlets. Traveller's equipment shone like silver. Officers, tears running down their cheeks, watched mutely. With a nod, a timid smile, Lee rode off for his rendezvous with Grant at Appomattox Court House.

Lee already had arrived when Grant and his staff reached the McLean farmhouse. "What General Lee's feelings were I do not know," Grant wrote in his *Memoirs*. "As he was a man of much dignity, it was impossible to say whether he felt inwardly glad, or felt sad and was too manly to show it. My own feelings, which had been quite jubilant on receipt of his letter, were sad and depressed." Grant, dusty and soiled in a loose fatigue coat, wore no side arms. The greetings between the two commanders were cordial, and Lee expressed his gratitude to General Williams, who had sent him a message that Custis, reported killed at Saylor's Creek, was unhurt.

Beneath the pleasant talk, Lee felt the strain. Finally he said to Grant: "General, I have come to meet you in accordance with my letter to you this morning, to treat about the surrender of my army, and I think the best way would be for you to put the terms in writing." Grant assented. On field notepaper that made its own copy at the time of writing, an aide wrote out the terms. Grant read the document and carried it across the room to Lee.

In this tense, sad moment Lee did the little things that heightened human drama—pushing aside some books and two brass candlesticks to give himself space at the table, drawing steel-rimmed spectacles from his pocket and wiping them carefully with his handkerchief, crossing his legs and adjusting his glasses before beginning to read. Once when he could find no pencil in his pocket to make a suggested insertion, Grant secured one for him. Throughout the remainder of the interview Lee twirled the pencil in his fingers or tapped the tabletop with it.

The portion of the surrender terms which stated that only public property was involved and officers could retain their side arms and personal baggage delighted Lee. "That will have a very happy effect," he told Grant. Then Lee added: "General, our cavalrymen furnish their own horses; they are not Government horses. Some of them may be, but of course you will find them out—

any property that is public property, you will ascertain that, but it is nearly all private property, and these men will want to plough ground and plant corn." He would give orders, Grant replied, that every man who claimed to own a horse or mule was to be allowed to take it home.

While Lee's reply was being drafted, Sheridan said to Colonel Marshall: "This is very pretty country."

Marshall smiled wryly. "General, I haven't seen it by daylight."

Sheridan laughed. Grant came over to the sofa. "Sheridan, how many rations have you?" Sheridan asked Grant how many he wanted. "General Lee has about a thousand or fifteen hundred of our people prisoners," Grant said, "and they are faring the same as his men, but he tells me his haven't anything. Can you spare them some rations?" Sheridan nodded. Would twenty-five thousand rations do? Grant asked Lee if that would be enough.

"Plenty, plenty," Lee replied. "An abundance."

Reading the draft of the reply, Lee was dissatisfied. "Don't say, 'have the honor to acknowledge the receipt of your letter of such a date'; he is here; just say, 'I accept these terms.'"

The two generals signed the papers. The ceremonies were brief and simple. Then Lee shook hands with Grant, bowed to the other officers, and left the room. Outside he saw the valley where his army lay—defeated, prisoners of war. Three times he struck the palm of his left hand with his right fist; he seemed to see no one else now, but to be lost somewhere within his own mind. An aide brought Traveller and the reverie vanished. Grant stepped down from the porch, moving toward Lee, raising his hat in salute. The other Union officers took off their hats. Lee returned the respectful gesture. Then, at a slow trot, he rode away.

In the valley, the army saw him returning, rushed to

the roadside, crowded around him, shook his hand—he was their grand old chief, and they cried out "Uncle Robert" and a few prayed: "God help you, General." Lee tried to speak. He could find only a few words:

"Men, we have fought through this war together. I have done the best I could for you. My heart is too full to say more."

And he rode on to his tent, to his sadness, to his heartbreak. Elsewhere in America church bells tolled. The day was Palm Sunday.

CHAPTER THIRTEEN

THE NOBLE LEE

THE LEE whom the South had found noble in war, the North judged to be noble in peace. The same wholeness of character and resolution that had carried Lee through four desperate years of struggle to Appomattox now led him back into years of gentle, unembittered determination to live by the bargain of his surrender. The journey began on April 12 when Lee, a paroled prisoner of war, mounted Traveller and turned toward home. News of his coming spread along the road; crowds gathered to see him, to wave, to cheer, to bring cooked provisions, to hold up babies named "Lee." Deeply touched, he said: "These good people are kind, too kind. Their hearts are as full as when we began our first campaigns in 1861. They do too much—more than they are able to do—for us." Wherever he stopped, he met the same respect and affection; at last, riding up through Manchester, he saw again the James and Richmond.

Suddenly Lee's heart felt constricted, for here clearly symbolized was the terrible price the South had paid for its Lost Cause: the bridges gone and stark, drab Federal pontoons in their place, the gutted, almost completely burned-out waterfront, the ruins of arsenal and factories, tobacco warehouses, and homes. Sadly he entered the city, riding uptown. And now the people came out to see him—the old gray warrior on the fine gray horse, sword at his side, head lifted proudly above a uniform that showed its long service—and tear-dimmed eyes gazed up at him, husky voices cried out in greeting, old veterans of a dozen battles cheered their "Uncle Robert," and Yankees came to the curb to watch and, caught up by the affecting scene, to doff their hats and honor "the grand old man." Lee pushed on doggedly, an old ambulance and a few tattered wagons rattling behind him. His eyes sought the doorway to "The Mess" at 707 East Franklin. Home—Mary and the children—to unbuckle his sword forever, to bury the old animosities and become anew a "loyal American" . . . these were parts of the vision he held.

With rest the aches of the last hard campaign began to fade. The family tried to cheer him, to ease the brittle memories. He seemed tired, so very, very tired, but he wanted to talk about anything except the war. People were forever calling, earnest that he should know their adoration for him—old soldiers with food, because they heard he was penniless; ministers to pray, wives to ask about husbands, and mothers about sons. Rob and his cousin Dan "formed a sort of guard of the young men in the house, some of whom took it by turns to keep the door, and, if possible, turn strangers away." Lee was too gentle and polite for his own good; never willingly would he turn anybody away, even a group of soldiers from the Virginia mountains who offered him a house and farm near a defile of rugged hills whence "they could defy the whole Federal army." Lee sent them away, tears in his eyes at their loyalty. But he had come to terms with his own heart and conscience: "I could have taken no other course save without dishonor." And now? The war had gone against the South—"it is the part of candor to recognize that fact and the part of wisdom to acquiesce in the result." One Sunday in church the congregation sat stunned when a Negro walked to the communion table; Lee knelt by the chancel rail, not far from the Negro, and the other communicants came forward, drawn by his example.

Officers, soldiers appealed to him as their commander-

in-chief; by word, by deed he gave them one answer—
to live scrupulously by the terms of parole. To Matthew
Fontaine Maury, later a scientist of renown, Lee wrote:

The thought of abandoning the country and all that must
be left in it is abhorrent to my feelings, and I prefer to struggle for its restoration and share its fate rather than to give up
all as lost. . . . Those citizens who can leave the country
and others who may be compelled to do so will reap the
benefits of your considerate labor; but I shall be very sorry
if your presence be lost to Virginia. She has now need for
all her sons and can ill afford to spare you. . . .

Another letter told Beauregard: "I am glad to see no indication in your letter of an intention to leave the country. I think the South requires the aid of her sons now
more than at any period of her history." And he argued:
"I need not tell you that true patriotism sometimes requires of men to act exactly contrary at one period to
that which it does at another, and the motive that impels
them—the desire to do right—is precisely the same."

Offers of many kinds poured in on Lee—to head a
New York firm promoting trade in the South at fifty
thousand dollars a year, to live on an estate in England
with an income of fifteen thousand dollars a year, the
gift of an admiring nobleman. In the first case his name
was "not for sale at any price"; in the other: "I must
abide the fortunes and share the fate of my people."
Young Rob grew impatient. "They are offering my father everything," he grumbled, "except the one thing he
will accept—a place to earn honest bread while engaged
in useful work." Lee's dream was of a small farm, a
chance to get Mary out of the city—"some little, quiet
place in the woods." Then the offer came from Lexington to be president of Washington College, closed since
the war. The salary was only fifteen hundred dollars a

year, and that the trustees had to borrow. Lee hesitated. Would his presence "draw upon the college a feeling of hostility"? But the trustees convinced him that quite the opposite result might be expected. Lee mounted Traveller and rode off on his last great adventure.

The years in Lexington were happy for Lee. The struggle to re-establish the college after the period of wartime impoverishment found him, characteristically, cheerful in the face of adversity. A campus was the perfect environment for his personality; here his unaffected sentimentality, his idealism, his fondness for little platitudes were positive assets. Young Rob saw him suddenly as "bright and even gay," laughing merrily "over difficulties that appalled the rest of us." From early morning until late night he worked with tremendous energy, a counselor to the faculty, a father to the students. Freshmen heard: "Young gentlemen, we have no printed rules. We have but one rule and it is that every student must be a gentleman." Falsehood and meanness were undergraduate offenses that he would not tolerate, but otherwise he was kind, mellow, lenient—a disciplinarian who had seen seemingly callow boys become heroes in the murky Wilderness, at Gettysburg, and in all the other battles he now tried to forget. A professor said of him: "To the faculty he was an elder brother, beloved and revered, and full of tender sympathy."

Each week, each month, absorbed in the work of the college, Lee more and more wished others to follow his example in putting the rancor of war behind them, yet even he could not escape the past. Going to Petersburg for Rooney's second marriage Lee fretted over the townspeople, whom he had been forced to abandon. Afterward from Lexington he wrote to Rooney: "My old feelings returned to me as I passed well-remembered spots and recalled the ravages of hostile shot and shell. But when I saw the cheerfulness with which the people were working to restore their fortunes, and witnessed the comforts with which they were surrounded, a cloud of sorrow which had been pressing upon me for years was lifted from my heart." Gamaliel Bradford told the wonderful story of a Confederate soldier who confessed to his officer that he had taken an oath of allegiance to the United States. "You have disgraced the family," the officer said. The soldier replied: "General Lee told me to do it." The officer laughed. "Oh, that alters the case. Whatever General Lee says is all right. I don't care what it is." Yet all bitterness could not be so quickly dispelled. A call from Pickett found both men cold and reserved and Pickett went away grumbling at "that old man" who "had my division massacred at Gettysburg." Dryly a third party commented: "Well, it made you immortal."

Lee's life settled more firmly into a gentle pattern, even though students at first glimpse were prone to be disappointed in him, arriving with preconceived notions of the great warrior's manliness and encountering instead, as one said, a college president who seemed "almost motherly." Perhaps Lee enjoyed this little shock; he had always liked to outwit "the enemy." He had likely experienced a few shocks of his own in Lexington, for a contemporary account of the institution described Washington College as "little more than a name"; the same spokesman enumerated the weaknesses of this "less than an efficient academy" with its "few students . . . buildings pillaged, defaced and falling into ruins . . . a slender faculty, and little endowment." But Lee saw the students come in increasing numbers, drawn by the magic of his name; the maintenance corps was set to work with hammer and paintbrush, for Lee loved orderliness; endowments trickled in, the college grew in prestige, and, said the earlier critic, delighted with the transformation, the growth, the busy campus: "Washington College took on the semblance of a great university, and began to be known as an institution of learning that was to be reckoned among the greater colleges."

But Lee always had possessed the ability of a first-rate administrator; he achieved what he had expected prudence and common sense and moral judgment always accomplished. He found time, as the college began to prosper, to give more of his attention to church affairs, always a ruling passion with him in the years before the war. Occasionally he might still be prodded into an opinion about the war, naming McClellan as the best general against whom he had fought (an opinion at which a great many modern historians will wince), but his mind kept shedding these memories, kept reaching back to a happier time. He sat for a bust of himself, more or less resigned to that chore; but his thoughts, his eagerness were whetted by the memoir of his father that he proposed to write. One day he reached for the manuscript, found a page, and read to a visitor lines by the Mussulman poet Hafiz that he had included:

> Learn from your Orient shell to love thy foe,
> And store with pearls the hand that brings thee woe;
> Free like yon rock, from base vindictive pride,
> Emblaze with gems the wrist that rends thy side:
> Mark where yon tree rewards the stony shower,
> With fruit nectareous, or balmy flower;
> All nature cries aloud, shall man do less
> Than heal the smiter and the railer bless?

Lee possessed a beautiful smile. Now, in the echoing from Arabia of this poet's voice of Shivaz, he found a philosophy to fit his own life. And he asked: "Ought not we who profess to be governed by the principles of

Christianity to rise at least to the standard of this Mohammedan poet and learn to forgive our enemies?" A bitter discussion on reconstruction, in which two professors had been heatedly engaged, ended.

All hoped that these pleasant years for Lee would long continue—for the good of the now flourishing college, for the discipline he exerted over still smoldering tempers in the South, for the charm and comfort that his presence gave to those who knew him as friend and counselor. Already he stood apart—a little more than mortal in the Southern mind—and we have the testimony of Professor James J. White, his closest friend in Lexington, that "no man was great enough to be intimate with General Lee." Yet Lee never encouraged this attitude. In the academic affairs of the college he made no pretense of great knowledge. In administrative matters he could be dogmatic, perhaps cussedly so; in education he listened more often to the opinions of the faculty. Naturally the professors wanted to please him: how else, from the president's point of view, does any college prosper?

A change came suddenly. The winter of 1869 brought a cold that continued to hang on and drove Lee finally, at his doctor's suggestion, to the milder climate of southern Georgia and Florida. Wherever he went, little girls appeared with their bouquets, mothers with more babies named "Lee," veterans sometimes on two legs and sometimes on one—he was still the hero. But his cold grew no better; pains developed in his chest and he went to Baltimore for a special examination; then he stayed only briefly in Lexington before going to Hot Springs to try the baths. In September, when he came back for the opening of another college year, he felt that "my pains are less and my strength greater."

But the old warrior was near the end. On September 28, 1870 he attended a vestry meeting of Grace Episcopal Church, sat through a damp, chilly afternoon wrapped in a military cape, then returning home to find his family at dinner, tried to say the evening prayer. His lips would not sound the words. He was laid on a couch. Except that he had not fainted he seemed to have concussion of the brain. When the family tried to remove his clothes, he complained: "You hurt my arm." Early October crept gently into Lexington. Custis spoke of an eventual recovery, but Lee shook his head. A doctor said: "You must make haste and get well; Traveller has been standing so long in the stable he needs exercise."

Mrs. Lee was wheeled in her chair to sit beside him. During these past few years at Lexington her invalidism had grown so bad that they had given up all social life. But Lee was content, having her near. One night he confessed a doubt: he always had tried to be a good Christian and wished he could feel sure of his acceptance. "All who love and trust in the Savior need not fear," Mary told him. Lee made no reply, and, looking down at his quiet face, Mary thought: "A more upright and conscientious Christian never lived."

On October 11 he began to sink—death a day away. "Tell Hill," he said once, emphatically, "he *must* come up!" And then, gently, he spoke his last words: "Strike the tent."

So did the mortal Lee follow Jackson across the last valley to rest under the shade of the trees. Another Lee, the hero of the Southern spirit, could not die. On the centennial of his birth throngs gathered in Richmond, and Charles Francis Adams, the speaker of the day, closed his tribute to Lee with an eloquent quotation from Carlyle:

Whom shall we consecrate and set apart as one of our sacred men? Sacred; that all men may see him, be reminded of him, and, by new example added to the old perpetual precept, be taught what is real worth in a man. Whom do you wish to resemble?

Above the speaker, carved in stone, sat Lee, mounted on Traveller.

A BIBLIOGRAPHICAL NOTE

LEE, at the time of his death, had begun to make notes and to collect data for an autobiography. This material was available to General A. L. Long in writing *Memoirs of Robert E. Lee* (New York, 1886). The years after the war, however, exacted a cruel toll from General Long; restricted by blindness, his work suffered for frequent flights into extraneous matters, for moments of querulous argumentation, for inaccuracies that more deliberate revision should have corrected, and yet the serious student of Lee reads Long for the wisdom he often sheds on the character and personality of his subject. In addition, four principal published sources of Lee's letters exist. First, of course, is Robert E. Lee, Jr.'s *Recollections and Letters of General Robert E. Lee* (New York, 1905), covering mainly that period in his father's life beginning in 1860; an enlarged edition, appearing in 1924, added nothing of importance to the original work. Other Lee letters of interest are to be found in Fitzhugh Lee's *General Lee* (New York, 1894); in J. William Jones's *Personal Reminiscences, Anecdotes and Letters of General Robert E. Lee* (New York, 1874); and in Avery Craven's editing of *To Markie* (Cambridge, 1933).

Among those who fought with Lee, these memoirs are of special value: E. P. Alexander: *Military Memoirs of a Confederate* (New York, 1907); Jubal A. Early: *Autobiographical Sketch and Narrative of the War Between the States* (Philadelphia, 1912); John B. Gordon: *Reminiscences of the Civil War* (New York, 1903); John B. Hood: *Advance and Retreat* (New Orleans, 1880); Joseph E. Johnston: *Narrative of Military Op-*

erations (New York, 1872); James Longstreet: *From Manassas to Appomattox* (Philadelphia, 1896), though scrutiny should be made of the review of this book which originally appeared in the *United Service Journal* and was reprinted in the *Southern Historical Society Papers* (Vol. XXXIX, p. 104); Charles Marshall: *An Aide-de-Camp to Lee* . . . edited by Major General Sir Frederick Maurice (Boston, 1927); and Richard Taylor: *Destruction and Reconstruction* (New York, 1879).

John Esten Cooke, who is quoted in these pages, produced highly valuable documents in *Wearing of the Gray* (New York, 1867) and *The Life of Stonewall Jackson* [by a Virginian] (Richmond, 1863). For an insight behind the scenes of official Richmond and the Confederacy, material has been drawn from J. B. Jones's fascinating *A Rebel War Clerk's Diary* (Philadelphia, 1866, 2 vols.) and chatty Mary Boykin Chesnut's *A Diary from Dixie* (New York, 1905, and Boston, 1949). Among foreign observers and participants particular insight was found in Heros von Borcke's *Memoirs of the Confederate War for Independence* (London, 1866, 2 vols.) and Lt. Col. A. J. L. Freemantle's *Three Months in the Southern States* (New York, 1864, and Boston, 1954). Perhaps the finest, and surely the most modest, of any American war memoir ever published is Ulysses S. Grant's *Personal Memoirs* (New York, 1885, 2 vols., and Cleveland and New York, 1952); for another engaging memoir this biographer is drawn repeatedly to Horace Porter's *Campaigning with Grant* (New York, 1897).

When one enters the realm of the eyewitness accounts of the Great Conflict, one should be forewarned that although this sea is balmy and seductive, it is apparently endless. Good collections exist, and volumes that will provide a fair start are *Annals of the War, Written by Leading Participants North and South* (Philadelphia, 1879), *Battles and Leaders of the Civil War* (New York, 1887-8, 4 vols.), the numerous volumes of the *Southern Historical Society Papers* (Richmond, beginning 1876), and the forty or more volumes of *Confederate Veteran* (Nashville, beginning 1893). Recent compilations of worthiness are Otto Eisenchiml and Ralph Newman: *The American Iliad* (Indianapolis, 1950) and Henry Steele Commager: *The Blue and the Gray* (Indianapolis, 1950). The more serious student likewise will turn often to *The War of the Rebellion: A Compilation of the Union and Confederate Armies,* more commonly cited as the *Official Records* (Washington, 1880-1901, 128 vols.); Frank Moore's edition of *The Rebellion Record* (New York, 1862-71, 12 vols.); the three parts of the *Report of the Joint Committee on the Conduct of the War* (Washington, 1863); and, for those especially engrossed in Lee's first major campaign, the U. S. General Staff School's *Source Book of the Peninsula Campaign in Virginia* (Fort Leavenworth, 1921).

The Introduction already has cited as the most authoritative biographical source available on Lee the four volumes of Douglas Southall Freeman's *R. E. Lee* (New York, 1935) and his three volumes of *Lee's Lieutenants* (New York, 1944). Commendable one-volume biographies have been written by Thomas Nelson Page (*Robert E. Lee, Man and Soldier,* New York, 1911), Henry A. White (*Robert E. Lee and the Southern Confederacy,* New York, 1897), and Robert W. Winston (*Robert E. Lee,* New York, 1934). The general reader who likes to focus many points of view upon his subject will enjoy Stanley F. Horn's *The Robert E. Lee Reader* (Indianapolis, 1949). A final word of indebtedness by all students to Dr. Freeman must be spoken for two other works: *A Calendar of Confederate Papers* (Richmond, 1908) and *Lee's Dispatches* (New York, 1915).

Any suggestive bibliographical note on Lee and his period must include Jefferson Davis's own *The Rise and Fall of the Confederate Government* (New York, 1881, 2 vols.), and mention should be made perhaps that Davis gave his estimate on Lee in an article in the *North American Review* (Vol. CL, No. 398, January 1890); also, reference is deserved by Varina Howell Davis's *Jefferson Davis . . . A Memoir by His Wife* (New York, 1890, 2 vols.) and Dunbar Rowland's selection and editing of *Jefferson Davis, Constitutionalist, His Letters, Papers and Speeches* (Jackson, 1923, 10 vols.).

Of the making of books about Lincoln, of course, there is still no end; a reliable, satisfying one-volume biography of the man and his times is Benjamin P. Thomas's *Abraham Lincoln* (New York, 1952). Another valuable source is *The Living Lincoln*, a one-volume edition in narrative form of his collected writings edited by Paul M. Angle and Earl Schenck Miers (New Brunswick, 1955).

In conclusion, it is only fair to warn the reader that subjects such as Lee, the war, Davis, Lincoln, are harbors leading to an ocean that will require a lifetime to explore. Many will testify that it is an exciting, exhilarating adventure. What, in effect, this note provides is the channel-markers to sail through the first of the "Narrows" that give entry to the route.

INDEX

A NOTE ON THE TYPE

This book was set on the Linotype in a face called *Eldorado*, so named by its designer, WILLIAM ADDISON DWIGGINS, as an echo of Spanish adventures in the Western World. The series of experiments that culminated in this type-face began in 1942; the designer was trying a page more "brunette" than the usual book type. "One wanted a face that should be sturdy, and yet not too mechanical. . . . Another desideratum was that the face should be narrowish, compact, and close fitted, for reasons of economy of materials." The specimen that started Dwiggins on his way was a type design used by the Spanish printer A. de Sancha at Madrid about 1774. Eldorado, however, is in no direct way a copy of that letter, though it does reflect the Madrid specimen in the anatomy of its arches, curves, and junctions. Of special interest in the lower-case letters are the stresses of color in the blunt, sturdy serifs, subtly counterbalanced by the emphatic weight of some of the terminal curves and finials. The roman capitals are relatively open, and winged with liberal serifs and an occasional festive touch.

This book was composed, printed, and bound by The Plimpton Press, Norwood, Massachusetts. Paper manufactured by S. D. Warren Company, Boston. The typography and binding were designed by the creator of its type-face—W. A. Dwiggins.